AF485427

The Mediterranean Cookbook

Explore the Abundance of Locally Grown Ingredients with Over 90 Recipes Inspired by the Mediterranean Diet

Luisa Vernizzi

Copyright © 2023 - All rights reserved.

The content contained within this book may not be reproduced, duplicated, or transmitted without direct written permission from the author or the publisher.

Under no circumstances will any blame or legal responsibility be held against the publisher, or author, for any damages, reparation, or monetary loss due to the information contained within this book. Either directly or indirectly.

Legal Notice:

This book is copyright protected. This book is only for personal use. You cannot amend, distribute, sell, use, quote, or paraphrase any part, or the content within this book, without the consent of the author or publisher.

Disclaimer Notice:

Please note the information contained within this document is for educational and entertainment purposes only. All effort has been executed to present accurate, up-to-date, and reliable, complete information. No warranties of any kind are declared or implied. Readers acknowledge that the author is not engaging in the rendering of legal, financial, medical, or professional advice. The content within this book has been derived from various sources. Please consult a licensed professional before attempting any techniques outlined in this book.

By reading this document, the reader agrees that under no circumstances is the author responsible for any losses, direct or indirect, which are incurred as a result of the use of the information contained within this document, including, but not limited to, — errors, omissions, or inaccuracies.

ISBN:

Table of Contents

Breakfast Recipes

1. Watermelon Pizza

Prep Time: 10 minutes

Cook Time: 0 minutes

Serving: 3

Ingredients

- 9 oz. watermelon slice
- 1 tablespoon Pomegranate sauce
- 2 oz. Feta cheese, crumbled
- 1 tablespoon fresh cilantro, chopped

Directions

1. Place the watermelon slice on a plate.

2. Sprinkle the crumbled Feta cheese over the watermelon slice.

3. Add the fresh cilantro on top.

4. Generously sprinkle the pizza with Pomegranate juice.

5. Cut the watermelon pizza into slices or servings as desired.

Nutrition: Calories 96, Fat 3.3 g, Protein 5 g, Carbohydrates 6.8 g, Sugar 6.1 g, Fiber 1 g

2. Cauliflower Fritters

Prep Time: 10 minutes

Cook Time: 10 minutes

Serving: 4

Ingredients

- 1 cup cauliflower, shredded
- 1 egg, beaten
- 1 tablespoon wheat flour, whole grain
- 1 oz. Parmesan, grated
- ½ teaspoon ground black pepper
- 1 tablespoon canola oil

Directions

1. In a mixing bowl, combine shredded cauliflower and an egg.
2. Add wheat flour, grated Parmesan cheese, and ground black pepper to the mixture.
3. Use a fork to stir the ingredients until they are well-mixed and smooth.
4. Heat canola oil in a skillet until it starts to boil.
5. Using your fingertips or a spoon, make fritters from the cauliflower mixture and transfer them to the hot oil.
6. Cook the fritters over medium-low heat for about 4 minutes on each side until they are golden brown and crispy.

Nutrition: Calories 83, Fat 6.3 g, Protein 5.9 g, Carbohydrates 3.3 g, Sugar 0.7 g, Fiber 0.8 g

3. Creamy Oatmeal with Figs

Prep Time: 10 minutes

Cook Time: 20 minutes

Serving: 5

Ingredients

- 2 cups oatmeal
- 1 ½ cup milk
- 1 tablespoon butter
- 3 figs, chopped
- 1 tablespoon honey

Directions

1. Pour milk into a saucepan.
2. Add oatmeal and cover with a lid.
3. Cook over medium-low heat for 15 minutes.
4. Add chopped figs and honey to the oatmeal.
5. Stir in the butter until it is fully incorporated.
6. Continue cooking for an additional 5 minutes.
7. Turn off the heat, cover the oatmeal with a lid, and let it rest for 10 minutes before serving it as a delicious breakfast.

Nutrition: Calories 222, fat 6 g, Protein 4.9 g, Carbohydrates 12 g, Sugar 12.5 g, Fiber 4.4 g

4. Baked Oatmeal with Cinnamon

Prep Time: 10 minutes

Cook Time: 25 minutes

Serving: 4

Ingredients

- 1 cup oatmeal
- 1/3 cup milk
- 1 pear, chopped
- 1 teaspoon vanilla extract
- 1 tablespoon Splenda
- 1 teaspoon butter

Directions

1. In a large bowl, combine oatmeal, milk, egg, vanilla extract, Splenda, and ground cinnamon.

2. Melt butter and add it to the oatmeal mixture. Mix well.

3. Add chopped pear to the mixture and stir until evenly distributed.

4. Transfer the oatmeal mixture to a casserole dish and flatten it gently. Cover the dish with foil, ensuring the edges are securely sealed.

5. Bake the oatmeal at 350F for 25 minutes.

Nutrition: Calories 134, Fat 4.69 g, Protein 4.3 g, Carbohydrates 23.3 g, Sugar 7.6 g, Fiber 3.2 g

5. Almond Chia Porridge

Prep Time: 10 minutes

Cook Time: 30 minutes

Serving: 4

Ingredients

- 3 cups organic almond milk
- 1/3 cup chia seeds, dried
- 1 teaspoon vanilla extract
- 1 tablespoon honey
- ¼ teaspoon ground cardamom

Directions

1. Pour almond milk into a saucepan and bring it to a boil.

2. Allow the almond milk to cool to room temperature (approximately 10-15 minutes).

3. Add vanilla extract, honey, and ground cardamom to the saucepan and stir well.

4. Add chia seeds to the mixture and stir again.

5. Cover the saucepan with a lid and let the chia seeds soak up the liquid for 20-25 minutes.

6. Transfer the prepared porridge into individual serving ramekins.

Nutrition: Calories 513, Fat 49 g, Protein 6.8 g, Carbohydrates 19.9 g, Sugar 10.5 g, Fiber 9.3 g

6. Berry Breakfast Smoothie

Prep Time: 3 minutes

Cook Time: 0 minute

Serving: 1

Ingredients

- 1/2 cup vanilla low-fat Greek yogurt
- 1/4 cup low-fat milk
- 1/2 cup blueberries or strawberries
- 6 to 8 ice cubes

Directions

Place the Greek yogurt, milk, and berries in a blender and blend until the berries are liquefied. Mix in ice cubes and blend on high. Serve immediately.

Nutrition: Calories 152, Fat 1.8 g, Protein 7.1 g, Carbohydrates 28 g, Sugar 24.9 g, Fiber 1.8 g

7. Mediterranean Omelet

Prep Time: 7 minutes
Cook Time: 12 minutes
Serving: 2

Ingredients

- 2 teaspoons olive oil
- 1 garlic clove
- 1/2 red bell pepper
- 1/2 yellow bell pepper
- 1/4 cup thinly sliced red onion
- 2 tablespoons chopped fresh basil
- 2 tablespoons chopped fresh parsley
- 1/2 teaspoon salt
- 1/2 teaspoon black pepper
- 4 large eggs, beaten

Directions

1. Heat 1 teaspoon of olive oil in a large skillet over medium heat.

2. Add one finely minced garlic clove, 1/2 sliced red bell pepper, 1/2 sliced yellow bell pepper, and 1/4 cup of thinly sliced red onion to the skillet. Sauté for about 5 minutes, frequently stirring.

3. Add 2 tablespoons of chopped fresh basil, 2 tablespoons of chopped fresh parsley, 1/2 teaspoon of salt, and 1/2 teaspoon of black pepper to the skillet. Increase the heat to medium-high and sauté for an additional 2 minutes.

4. Transfer the vegetable mixture onto a plate and return the skillet to heat.

5. Add 1 teaspoon of olive oil to the skillet and pour in 4 beaten eggs, tilting the skillet to coat the bottom evenly. Cook until the edges are bubbly and all but the center is dry about 3 to 5 minutes.

6. Flip the omelet or use a spatula to turn it over.

7. Spoon the vegetable mixture onto one-half of the omelet and use a spatula to fold the other half over the top.

8. Slide the omelet onto a platter or cutting board, and cut it in half.

9. Garnish with fresh parsley and serve.

Nutrition: Calories 204, Fat 14.8 g, Protein 13.4 g, Carbohydrates 5.5 g, Sugar 2.9 g, Fiber 1.1 g

8. Hearty Berry Breakfast Oats

Prep Time: 11 minutes

Cook Time: 2 minutes

Serving: 2

Ingredients

- 11/2 cups whole-grain rolled oats
- ¾ cup fresh blueberries, raspberries, or blackberries, or a combination
- 2 teaspoons honey
- 2 tablespoons walnut pieces

Directions

1. Cook the whole-grain oats according to the instructions on the package and evenly divide them into 2 deep bowls.

2. In a small bowl that is safe for microwave use, heat the berries and honey for 30 seconds. Add the fruit mixture on top of each bowl of oatmeal. Then, sprinkle the walnuts over the fruit and serve while hot.

Nutrition: Calories 179, Fat 7.2 g, Protein 5.6 g, Carbohydrates 28.9 g, Sugar 6.8 g, Fiber 3.9 g

9. Garden Scramble

Prep Time: 9 minutes

Cook Time: 13 minutes

Serving: 4

Ingredients

- 1 teaspoon olive oil
- 1/2 cup diced yellow squash
- 1/2 cup diced green bell pepper
- 1/4 cup diced sweet white onion
- 6 cherry tomatoes, halved
- 1 tablespoon chopped fresh basil
- 1 tablespoon chopped fresh parsley
- 1/2 teaspoon salt
- 1/4 teaspoon freshly ground black pepper
- 8 large eggs, beaten

Directions

1. In a large skillet, heat the olive oil over medium heat.

2. Add the yellow squash, green bell pepper, and sweet white onion to the skillet and sauté for 5-7 minutes until the vegetables are tender.

3. Add the cherry tomatocs, basil, parsley, salt, and black pepper to the skillet and stir well.

4. Cook for another 2-3 minutes, occasionally stirring.

5. Pour the beaten eggs into the skillet and gently stir until the eggs are fully cooked and scrambled, about 3-5 minutes.

6. Serve hot, and enjoy!

Nutrition: Calories 197, Fat 11.6 g, Protein 14.7 g, Carbohydrates 10.4 g, Sugar 6.8 g, Fiber 2.8 g

10. Summer Day Fruit Salad

Prep Time: 16 minutes

Cook Time: 0-minute

Serving: 8

Ingredients

- 2 cups cubed honeydew melon
- 2 cups cubed cantaloupe
- 2 cups red seedless grapes
- 1 cup sliced fresh strawberries
- 1 cup fresh blueberries
- Zest and juice of 1 large lime

Directions

1. Wash and prepare all the fruits as needed. Cube the honeydew melon and cantaloupe into bite-sized pieces. Slice the strawberries.

2. In a large bowl, combine the cubed honeydew melon, cantaloupe, and red seedless grapes.

3. Add the sliced strawberries and fresh blueberries to the bowl.

4. Zest the lime and add it to the bowl.

5. Cut the zested lime in half and squeeze the juice over the fruit.

6. Gently toss all the ingredients together until the fruit is evenly coated with the lime juice and zest.

7. Cover the bowl with plastic wrap and refrigerate for at least 30 minutes before serving.

8. Serve the fruit salad chilled and garnish with additional lime zest or fresh mint leaves if desired.

Nutrition: Calories 67, Fat 0.1 g, Protein 0.8 g, Carbohydrates 17 g, Sugar 14.2 g, Fiber 3.8 g

11. Peach Sunrise Smoothie

Prep Time: 6 minutes

Cook Time: 0-minute

Serving: 2

Ingredients

- 1 large unpeeled peach, pitted and sliced (about 1/2 cup)
- 6 ounces vanilla or peach low-fat Greek yogurt
- 2 tablespoons low-fat milk
- 6 to 8 ice cubes

Directions

1. Add the sliced peach, Greek yogurt, low-fat milk, and ice cubes to a blender.

2. Blend the ingredients until smooth and creamy.

3. If the smoothie is too thick, add a little more milk or water to thin it out.

4. Pour the smoothie into a glass and enjoy!

Nutrition: Calories 106, Fat 0.4 g, Protein 6.7 g, Carbohydrates 19.8 g, Sugar 16.8 g, Fiber 1.2 g

12. Oat and Fruit Parfait

Prep Time: 11 minutes

Cook Time: 0-minute

Serving: 2

Ingredients

- 1/2 cup whole-grain rolled oats
- 1/2 cup walnut pieces
- 1 teaspoon honey
- 1 cup sliced fresh strawberries
- 11/2 cups (12 ounces) vanilla low-fat Greek yogurt
- Fresh mint leaves for garnish

Directions

1. Preheat the oven to 350°F.

2. Spread the rolled oats and walnut pieces on a baking sheet and bake for 10 to 12 minutes or until lightly toasted and fragrant. Remove from the oven and let cool.

3. In a small bowl, mix the toasted oats and walnuts with honey until evenly coated.

4. To assemble the parfait, spoon a layer of the oat and walnut mixture into the bottom of a glass or jar. Top with a layer of sliced strawberries, followed by a layer of Greek yogurt.

5. Repeat layering until all the ingredients are used up, ending with a layer of Greek yogurt on top.

6. Garnish with fresh mint leaves and immediately serve, or cover and refrigerate until ready to serve.

Nutrition: Calories 463, Fat 21.1 g, Protein 23.4 g, Carbohydrates 48.8 g, Sugar 25.4 g, Fiber 6.2 g

13. Savory Avocado Spread

Prep Time: 17 minutes

Cook Time: 0-minute

Serving: 4

Ingredients

- 1 ripe avocado
- 1 teaspoon lemon juice
- 6 boneless sardine filets
- 1/4 cup diced sweet white onion
- 1 stalk celery, diced
- 1/2 teaspoon salt
- 1/4 teaspoon black pepper

Directions

1. Cut the avocado in half, remove the pit, and scoop the flesh into a medium mixing bowl.

2. Add the lemon juice to the bowl and use a fork to mash the avocado and lemon juice together until smooth.

3. Drain the sardines and add them to the avocado mixture.

4. Mash the sardines and avocado with a fork until well combined.

5. Add the diced onion, celery, salt, and black pepper to the mixture and stir until evenly distributed.

6. Transfer the avocado spread to a serving bowl and serve immediately with your choice of crackers, bread, or vegetables.

Nutrition: Calories 126, Fat 9.46 g, Protein 5.6 g, Carbohydrates 6.18 g, Sugar 1.46 g, Fiber 3.7 g

14. Fresh Tomato Pasta Bowl

Prep Time: 7 minutes

Cook Time: 26 minutes

Serving: 4

Ingredients

- 8 ounces whole-grain linguine
- 1 tablespoon extra-virgin olive oil
- 2 garlic cloves, minced
- 1/4 cup chopped yellow onion
- 1 teaspoon chopped fresh oregano
- 1/2 teaspoon salt
- 1/4 teaspoon freshly ground black pepper
- 1 teaspoon tomato paste
- 8 ounces cherry tomatoes, halved
- 1/2 cup grated Parmesan cheese
- 1 tablespoon chopped fresh parsley

Directions

1. Cook the linguine according to the package instructions.

2. While the linguine is cooking, heat the olive oil in a large skillet over medium heat.

3. Add the minced garlic and chopped onion to the skillet and sauté for 3-5 minutes, until softened and fragrant.

4. Add the chopped oregano, salt, black pepper, and tomato paste to the skillet and stir to combine.

5. Add the cherry tomatoes to the skillet and cook for 5-7 minutes until they begin to soften and release their juices.

6. Drain the cooked linguine and add it to the skillet with the tomato sauce.

7. Toss the linguine and sauce together until well combined.

8. Add the grated Parmesan cheese to the skillet and toss again.

9. Divide the pasta between four serving bowls and garnish each with chopped fresh parsley before serving.

Nutrition: Calories 159, Fat 3.87 g, Protein 4.51 g, Carbohydrates 27.9 g, Sugar 4.04 g, Fiber 2.8 g

15. Garlicky Broiled Sardines

Prep Time: 6 minutes

Cook Time: 31 minutes

Serving: 4

Ingredients

- 4 (3.25-ounce) cans sardines packed in water or olive oil
- 2 tablespoons extra-virgin olive oil
- 4 garlic cloves, minced
- 1/2 teaspoon red pepper flakes
- 1/2 teaspoon salt
- 1/4 teaspoon black pepper

Directions

1. Preheat the broiler.
2. Drain the sardines and pat them dry with paper towels.
3. Arrange the sardines in a single layer on a broiler pan.
4. In a small bowl, combine the olive oil, minced garlic, red pepper flakes, salt, and black pepper.
5. Brush the mixture evenly over the sardines.
6. Broil the sardines for 3-4 minutes or until heated through and slightly browned.
7. Serve immediately.

Nutrition: Calories 223, Fat 13.5 g, Protein 22.8 g, Carbohydrates 1.13 g, Sugar 0.05 g, Fiber 0.1 g

16. Heart-Healthful Trail Mix

Prep Time: 8 minutes
Cook Time: 32 minutes
Serving: 12

Ingredients

- 1 cup raw almonds
- 1 cup walnut halves
- 1 cup pumpkin seeds
- 1 cup dried apricots, cut into thin strips
- 1 cup dried cherries, roughly chopped
- 1 cup golden raisins
- 2 tablespoons extra-virgin olive oil
- 1 teaspoon salt

Directions

1. Preheat the oven to 350°F (175°C).

2. Spread the almonds, walnuts, and pumpkin seeds on a baking sheet in a single layer.

3. Roast the nuts and seeds in the preheated oven for 10-12 minutes, occasionally stirring, until lightly toasted and fragrant.

4. Remove the baking sheet from the oven and let the nuts and seeds cool to room temperature.

5. In a large mixing bowl, combine the toasted nuts and seeds with the dried apricots, dried cherries, and golden raisins.

6. Drizzle the extra-virgin olive oil over the trail mix and sprinkle with salt.

7. Toss the ingredients together until well combined and evenly coated.

8. Store the trail mix in an airtight container at room temperature for up to 1 month.

Nutrition: Calories 185, Fat 10.3 g, Protein 4.9 g, Carbohydrates 21.9 g, Sugar 15 g, Fiber 2.7 g

17. Citrus-Kissed Melon

Prep Time: 11 minutes

Cook Time: 0-minute

Serving: 4

Ingredients

- 2 cups cubed melon
- 2 cups cubed cantaloupe
- 1/2 cup freshly squeezed orange juice
- 1/4 cup freshly squeezed lime juice
- 1 tablespoon orange zest

Directions

1. In a large bowl, combine the cubed melon and cantaloupe.

2. In a separate bowl, whisk together the freshly squeezed orange juice, lime juice, and orange zest.

3. Pour the citrus mixture over the melon and toss gently to coat.

4. Cover the bowl and refrigerate for at least 30 minutes before serving.

Nutrition: Calories 81, Fat 0.39 g, Protein 1.79 g, Carbohydrates 19.7 g, Sugar 17.5 g, Fiber 1.7 g

18. Café Cooler

Prep Time: 16 minutes

Cook Time: 0-minutes

Serving: 4

Ingredients

- Ice cubes
- 2 cups low-fat milk
- 1/2 teaspoon ground cinnamon
- 1/2 teaspoon pure vanilla extract
- 1 cup espresso, cooled to room temperature

Directions

1. Fill a blender with ice cubes.

2. Pour low-fat milk into the blender.

3. Add ground cinnamon and pure vanilla extract.

4. Pour cooled espresso into the blender.

5. Blend the mixture until smooth and frothy.

6. Pour the Café Cooler into glasses and immediately serve.

Nutrition: Calories 214, Fat 14.3 g, Protein 18.79 g, Carbohydrates 1.79 g, Sugar 0.44 g, Fiber 0.2 g

19. Smoked Salmon Appetizer with Fresh Cucumber

Prep Time: 10 minutes

Cook Time: 0-minute

Serving: 4

Ingredients

- 2 ½ tbsp. sour cream 10%
- 16 slices rye bread
- 3 tbsp. Greek yogurt
- Dill to taste
- 16 pieces smoked salmon
- 16 pieces' cucumbers

Directions

1. In a small mixing bowl, combine 2 1/2 tablespoons of 10% sour cream and 3 tablespoons of Greek yogurt. Mix well.

2. Add dill to the mixture according to taste and mix again.

3. Cut 16 slices of rye bread into small pieces, around 2 inches by 2 inches.

4. Place a piece of smoked salmon on top of each bread piece.

5. Cut 16 slices of cucumber into thin rounds and place one piece on top of each salmon slice.

6. Spoon a small amount of the sour cream and yogurt mixture on top of each cucumber slice.

7. Garnish with additional dill if desired.

8. Serve chilled.

Nutrition: Calories 452, Fat 8.3 g, Protein 27 g, Carbohydrates 66 g, Sugar 15.3 g, Fiber 11.4 g

20. Cypriot Tomato Salad

Prep Time: 13 minutes

Cook Time: 0-minute

Serving: 4

Ingredients

- 4 pieces' tomatoes
- 50 ml sesame oil
- 1 tbsp. red wine vinegar
- 2 tbsp. - dried oregano
- coarse sea salt to taste
- 9 Oz feta cheese

Directions

1. Wash and dice the tomatoes into small pieces, removing the seeds.

2. In a small mixing bowl, whisk the sesame oil, red wine vinegar, and dried oregano to make the dressing.

3. Add the diced tomatoes to a serving bowl and pour the dressing over the top. Toss gently to evenly coat the tomatoes.

4. Crumble the feta cheese over the top of the tomato mixture, and sprinkle with coarse sea salt to taste.

5. Chill the salad for at least 30 minutes to allow the flavors to meld together, then serve and enjoy.

Nutrition: Calories 286, Fat 26 g, Protein 9.39 g, Carbohydrates 4.08 g, Sugar 3.38 g, Fiber 0.5 g

Lunch Recipes

21. Baked Fish with Tomatoes and Mushrooms

Prep Time: 12 minutes

Cook Time: 25 minutes

Serving: 4

Ingredients

- Fish (4, whole and small, 12 oz. each)
- Salt (to taste) - Pepper (to taste)
- Dried thyme (pinch)
- Parsley (4 sprigs)
- Olive oil (as needed)
- Onion (4 oz., small dice)
- Shallots (1 oz., minced)
- Mushrooms (8 oz., chopped)
- Tomato concussed (6.4 oz.)
- Dry white wine (3.2 FL oz.)

Directions

1. Clean and scale the small whole fish, leaving the heads on. Season the inside and outside of the fish with salt and pepper. Add a pinch of dried thyme and a sprig of parsley in the cavity of each fish.

2. Use enough baking pans to hold the fish in a single layer. Brush the pans with a little olive oil.

3. In a pan, sauté the diced onions and minced shallots in a little olive oil for about 1 minute.

4. Add the chopped mushrooms and sauté for a few minutes.

5. Spread the sautéed vegetables and concussed tomatoes in the bottom of the baking pans.

6. Place the seasoned fish on top of the vegetables in the pans. Brush the tops lightly with olive oil. Pour the white wine into the pans.

7. Bake in a preheated oven at 400F for 15-20 minutes.

8. Remove the baked fish from the pans and keep them warm.

9. Remove the vegetables from the pans with a slotted spoon and adjust the seasoning if necessary. Serve a spoonful of vegetables with each fish, placing it under or alongside the fish.

10. Strain and skim the fat from the cooking liquid. Reduce the liquid slightly. Before serving, moisten each portion of fish with 1-2 tablespoons of the cooking liquid.

Nutrition: Calories 225, Fat 0.8 g, Protein 16 g, Carbohydrates 26 g, Sugar 4.8 g, Fiber 1.8 g

22. Goat Cheese and Walnut Salad

Prep Time: 15 minutes

Cook Time: 10 minutes

Serving: 3

Ingredients

- Beet (2 oz.)
- Arugula (3 oz.)
- Bibb lettuce (2 oz.)
- Romaine lettuce (9 oz.)
- Breadcrumbs (1/4 cup, dry)
- Dried thyme (1/4 tbsp.)
- Dried basil (1/4 tbsp.)
- Black pepper (1/3 tsp.)
- Fresh goat's milk cheese (6.35 oz., preferably in log shape)
- Walnut pieces (1.1 oz.)
- Red wine vinaigrette (2 fl. Oz.)

Directions

1. Prepare the salad greens by trimming, washing, and drying them.

2. Tear the greens into small pieces and toss them in a bowl.

3. Combine the dried thyme, basil, black pepper, and breadcrumbs in a separate bowl.

4. Slice the goat's milk cheese into 1 oz pieces, and roll them in the seasoned crumbs to coat.

5. Place the coated cheese pieces on a sheet pan and bake at 425 F for 10 minutes.

6. While the cheese is baking, toast the walnut pieces in a dry sauté pan or the oven.

7. Toss the greens with the red wine vinaigrette and arrange them on cold plates. Top each plate of greens with 2 pieces of baked cheese and sprinkle with toasted walnuts.

Nutrition: Calories 480, Fat 38 g, Protein 23 g, Carbohydrates 16 g, Sugar 5.22 g, Fiber 6.1 g

23. Tomato Tea Party Sandwiches

Prep Time: 15 minutes

Cook Time: 0-minute

Serving: 4

Ingredients

- Whole wheat bread (4 slices)
- Extra virgin olive oil (4 1/3 tbsp.)
- Basil (2 1/8 tbsp., minced)
- Tomato slices (4 thick)
- Ricotta cheese (4 oz.)
- Dash of pepper

Directions

1. Toast 4 slices of whole wheat bread to your desired level of toasting.

2. Spread 1 tablespoon plus 1 teaspoon of extra virgin olive oil evenly over each slice of toasted bread.

3. Spread 1 oz. of ricotta cheese on top of the oiled bread slices.

4. Place a thick slice of tomato on top of the cheese.

5. Sprinkle each slice with 1/2 tablespoon of minced basil and a dash of pepper.

6. Serve the toast with a glass of lemon water, and enjoy!

Nutrition: Calories 194, Fat 7.8 g, Protein 7.4 g, Carbohydrates 25 g, Sugar 2.5 g, Fiber 3.1 g

24. Veggie Shish Kebabs

Prep Time: 10 minutes

Cook Time: 0-minute

Serving: 3

Ingredients
- Cherry tomatoes (9)
- Mozzarella balls (9 low-fat)
- Basil leaves (9)
- Olive oil (1 tsp.)
- Zucchini (3, sliced)
- Dash of pepper

For Serving:
- Whole Wheat Bread (6 slices)

Directions
1. Thread one cherry tomato, one-low-fat mozzarella ball, one slice of zucchini, and one basil leaf onto each skewer.

2. Arrange the skewers on a plate and drizzle with olive oil. Sprinkle with a dash of pepper.

3. Toast the bread slices.

4. Serve two slices of toasted bread with three skewers each.

Nutrition: Calories 134, Fat 1.5 g, Protein 27.4 g, Carbohydrates 4.5 g, Sugar 2.37 g, Fiber 1.9g

25. Crispy Falafel

Prep Time: 20 minutes

Cook Time: 8 minutes

Serving: 3

Ingredients

- Chickpeas (1 cup, drained and rinsed)
- Parsley (½ cup, chopped with stems removed)
- Cilantro (1/3 cup, chopped with stems removed)
- Dill (¼ cup, chopped with stems removed)
- Cloves garlic (4, minced)
- Sesame seeds (1 tbsp., toasted)
- Coriander (½ tbsp.)
- Black pepper (½ tbsp.)
- Cumin (½ tbsp.)
- Baking powder (½ tsp.)
- Cayenne (½ tsp.)

Directions

1. Use a paper towel to thoroughly dry the chickpeas.

2. In a food processor, pulse together the parsley, cilantro, and dill until finely chopped.

3. In a mixing bowl, combine the chickpeas, minced garlic, coriander, black pepper, cumin, baking powder, and cayenne.

4. Add the herb mixture to the chickpea mixture and stir until well combined.

5. Transfer the mixture to an airtight container and chill in the refrigerator for at least 1 hour.

6. Remove the mixture from the refrigerator and mix in the toasted sesame seeds and additional baking powder, if desired.

7. Heat about 3 inches of olive oil in a pan over medium heat.

8. Use a tablespoon to scoop the mixture and form 12 patties, flattening each one slightly.

9. Fry the patties in the hot oil for 1-2 minutes on each side or until golden brown.

10. Use a slotted spoon to transfer the falafel patties to a plate lined with paper towels to drain excess oil.

11. Serve hot and enjoy with your favorite dipping sauce or in a pita sandwich.

Nutrition: Calories 114, Fat 1.5 g, Protein 5.6 g, Carbohydrates 17.7 g, Sugar 2.75 g, Fiber 5 g

26. Tuna Tartare

Prep Time: 15 minutes

Cook Time: 0-minute

Serving: 2

Ingredients

- Sashimi quality tuna (26.5 g, well-trimmed)
- Shallots (1 oz., minced)
- Parsley (2 tbsp., chopped)
- Fresh tarragon (2 tbsp., chopped)
- Lime juice (2 tbsp.)
- Dijon-style mustard (1 FL oz.)
- Olive oil (2 FL oz.)

Directions

1. Use a sharp knife to finely chop the tuna into small pieces.

2. In a bowl, mix the minced shallots, chopped parsley, chopped tarragon, lime juice, Dijonstyle mustard, and olive oil.

3. Add the chopped tuna to the bowl and mix everything until well combined.

4. Using a ring mold, carefully shape the tuna tartare into a round shape on a plate.

5. Season to taste with salt and pepper.

6. Serve immediately and enjoy!

Nutrition: Calories 290, Fat 28 g, Protein 4.7 g, Carbohydrates 6.29 g, Sugar 1.66 g, Fiber 1.4 g

27. Grilled Vegetable Kebabs

Prep Time: 12 minutes

Cook Time: 13 minutes

Serving: 6

Ingredients

- Zucchini (6 oz., trimmed)
- Yellow Summer Squash (6 oz., trimmed)
- Bell pepper (6 oz., red or orange, cut into 1 ½ in. squares)
- Onion (12 oz., red, large dice)
- Mushroom caps (12, medium)
- Olive oil (12 FL oz.)
- Garlic (1/2 oz., crushed)
- Rosemary (1 ½ tsp, dried)
- Thyme (1/2 tsp., dried)
- Salt (2 tsps.)
- Black pepper (1/2 tsp.)

Directions

1. Cut the trimmed zucchini and yellow squash into 12 slices each, making a total of 24 slices.

2. Thread the zucchini, yellow squash, red/orange bell pepper, onion, and mushroom caps onto 12 bamboo skewers, ensuring that each skewer has an even amount of vegetables.

3. Place the skewers in a single layer in a hotel pan.

4. In a separate bowl, combine the olive oil, crushed garlic, dried rosemary, dried thyme, salt, and black pepper to make the marinade.

5. Pour the marinade over the vegetable skewers, ensuring all vegetables are coated. Turn the skewers once or twice during the marination process to ensure the vegetables are evenly coated.

6. Marinate for 1 hour.

7. Remove the vegetable skewers from the marinade and allow any excess oil to drip off before grilling or roasting.

Nutrition: Calories 520, Fat 54 g, Protein 1.57 g, Carbohydrates 9.8 g, Sugar 5.56 g, Fiber 1.9 g

28. Marinated Feta and Artichokes

Prep Time: 10 minutes + 4 hours

Cook Time: 0 minute

Serving: 3

Ingredients

- 4 ounces traditional Greek feta, cut into ½-inch cubes
- 4 ounces drained artichoke hearts, quartered lengthwise
- 1/3 cup extra-virgin olive oil
- Zest and juice of 1 lemon
- 2 tablespoons roughly chopped fresh rosemary
- 2 tablespoons roughly chopped fresh parsley
- ½ teaspoon black peppercorns

Directions

1. In a bowl, gently mix the cubed feta and quartered artichoke hearts.

2. Add the olive oil, lemon zest, juice, chopped rosemary, parsley, and black peppercorns. Carefully toss the ingredients together to coat the feta and artichoke hearts without breaking them.

3. Cover the bowl and refrigerate for at least 4 hours to allow the flavors to meld.

4. When ready to serve, take the bowl out of the fridge and allow it to sit at room temperature for a few minutes before serving.

Nutrition: Calories186, Fat 14 g, Protein 8 g, Carbohydrates 6.33 g, Sugar 0.8 g, Fiber 3.5 g

29. Smoked Salmon Crudités

Prep Time: 10 minutes

Cook Time: 0-minute

Serving: 4

Ingredients

- 6 ounces smoked wild salmon
- 2 tablespoons Roasted Garlic Aioli
- 1 tablespoon Dijon mustard
- 1 tablespoon chopped scallions
- 2 teaspoons chopped capers
- ½ teaspoon dried dill
- 4 endive spears or hearts of romaine
- ½ English cucumber

Directions

1. Begin by cutting the smoked salmon into small pieces. Then, mix the smoked salmon with Roasted Garlic Aioli, Dijon mustard, chopped scallions, capers, and dried dill in a bowl.

2. Take endive spears or hearts of romaine and place a spoonful of the smoked salmon mixture on top of each one. Alternatively, slice the English cucumber into rounds and place a spoonful of the mixture on each one.

3. Chill the prepared endive spears/romaine hearts and cucumber rounds for a refreshing and delicious appetizer.

Nutrition: Calories 179, Fat 4.75 g, Protein 18 g, Carbohydrates 19.3 g, Sugar 1.76 g, Fiber 16 g

30. Olive Tapenade with Anchovies

Prep Time: 70 minutes

Cook Time: 0-minute

Serving: 4

Ingredients

- 2 cups pitted Kalamata olives
- 2 anchovy fillets
- 2 teaspoons capers
- 1 garlic clove
- 1 cooked egg yolk
- 1 teaspoon Dijon mustard
- ¼ cup extra-virgin olive oil

Directions

1. Rinse the Kalamata olives under cold water and drain them thoroughly.

2. Combine the olives, anchovy fillets, capers, garlic clove, cooked egg yolk, and Dijon mustard in a food processor.

3. Process the ingredients until they are well combined and form a coarse paste.

4. While the processor is running, slowly drizzle in the extra-virgin olive oil until the mixture is smooth.

5. Cover the olive tapenade and refrigerate it for at least one hour before serving.

6. Enjoy the tapenade with Seedy Crackers or your preferred dipper.

Nutrition: Calories 150, Fat 14 g, Protein 2.0 g, Carbohydrates 4.89 g, Sugar 0.06 g, Fiber 2.4 g

31. Zucchini-Ricotta Fritters with Lemon-Garlic Aioli

Prep Time: 30 minute

Cook Time: 25 minutes

Serving: 4

Ingredients

- 1 large zucchini
- 1 teaspoon salt, divided
- ½ cup whole-milk ricotta cheese
- 2 scallions
- 1 large egg
- 2 garlic cloves
- 2 tablespoons fresh mint (optional)
- 2 teaspoons grated lemon zest
- ¼ teaspoon freshly ground black pepper
- ½ cup almond flour
- 1 teaspoon baking powder
- 8 tablespoons extra-virgin olive oil
- 8 tablespoons Roasted Garlic Aioli

Directions

1. Begin by preparing the zucchini. Place the shredded zucchini in a colander or on several layers of paper towels and sprinkle with ½ teaspoon of salt. Let it sit for 10 minutes, then use another layer of paper towel to press down on the zucchini and release any excess moisture. Pat it dry and set it aside.

2. In a mixing bowl, combine the drained zucchini, ricotta cheese, scallions, egg, garlic, mint (if using), lemon zest, remaining ½-teaspoon salt, and pepper. Stir everything together until well combined.

3. In a separate bowl, mix the almond flour and baking powder. Add the flour mixture to the zucchini mixture and stir until everything is fully incorporated. Let the mixture rest for 10 minutes.

4. Heat 2 tablespoons of olive oil in a large skillet over medium-high heat. Use a heaping tablespoon of the zucchini batter per fritter and press it down with the back of a spoon to form 2- to 3-inch fritters. Cook for 2 minutes covered, flip the fritters, and cook for another 2-3 minutes until both sides are golden brown. Repeat this process with the remaining batter and olive oil, working in four batches.

5. Once all the fritters are cooked, serve them with the Roasted Garlic Aioli on the side.

Nutrition: Calories 313, Fat 20.1 g, Protein 6.96 g, Carbohydrates 27.77 g, Sugar 16.54 g, Fiber 1.9 g

32. Salmon-Stuffed Cucumbers

Prep Time: 10 minutes

Cook Time: 0-minute

Serving: 4

Ingredients

- 2 large cucumbers, peeled
- 1 (4-ounce) can red salmon
- 1 medium very ripe avocado
- 1 tablespoon extra-virgin olive oil
- Zest and juice of 1 lime
- 3 tablespoons chopped fresh cilantro
- ½ teaspoon salt
- ¼ teaspoon black pepper

Directions

1. Peel and slice cucumbers into 1-inch-thick segments. Use a spoon to scrape the seeds out of the center of each segment and then stand them up on a plate.

2. In a medium bowl, combine the canned salmon, very ripe avocado (mashed or diced), extra-virgin olive oil, lime zest and juice, chopped cilantro, salt, and black pepper. Mix until well combined.

3. Spoon the salmon mixture into the center of each cucumber segment, filling it to the top.

4. Once all the cucumbers are stuffed, chill them in the refrigerator for at least 30 minutes before serving. This will

allow the flavors to meld together and make the dish more refreshing.

Nutrition: Calories 212, Fat 12.35 g, Protein 19.11 g, Carbohydrates 8.38 g, Sugar 2.4 g, Fiber 4.5 g

33. Goat Cheese–Mackerel Pâté

Prep Time: 10 minutes

Cook Time: 0 minute

Serving: 4

Ingredients

- 4 ounces olive oil-packed wild-caught mackerel
- 2 ounces goat cheese
- Zest and juice of 1 lemon
- 2 tablespoons chopped fresh parsley
- 2 tablespoons chopped fresh arugula
- 1 tablespoon extra-virgin olive oil
- 2 teaspoons chopped capers
- 2 teaspoons fresh horseradish (optional)

Directions

1. Combine the olive oil-packed wild-caught mackerel, goat cheese, lemon zest and juice, chopped parsley, chopped arugula, extra-virgin olive oil, capers, and fresh horseradish (if using) in a food processor, blender, or large bowl with an immersion blender.

2. Process or blend the ingredients together until they are smooth and creamy.

3. Once the pâté is blended to your desired texture, transfer it to a serving dish.

4. Serve the goat cheese-mackerel pâté with crackers, cucumber rounds, endive spears, celery, or any other accompaniment of your choice.

5. Enjoy the flavors of the Mediterranean in this quick and easy recipe that can be served as a healthy snack or appetizer.

Nutrition: Calories 186, Fat 18.01 g, Protein 4.76 g, Carbohydrates 1.91 g, Sugar 0.87 g, Fiber 0.4 g

34. Tuscan Kale Salad with Anchovies

Prep Time: 45 minutes

Cook Time: 0-minute

Serving: 4

Ingredients

- 1 large bunch Lacinato
- ¼ cup toasted pine nuts
- 1 cup Parmesan cheese
- ¼ cup extra-virgin olive oil
- 8 anchovy fillets
- 2 to 3 tablespoons lemon juice
- 2 teaspoons red pepper flakes (optional)

Directions

1. Remove the center stems from the kale leaves and tear them into strips of roughly 4-by-1 inches. Place the torn kale in a large bowl and add the toasted pine nuts and Parmesan cheese.

2. In a blender or food processor, combine the extra-virgin olive oil, anchovy fillets, lemon juice, and red pepper flakes (if using). Blend until smooth, and pour the mixture over the salad. Toss well to ensure that the salad is evenly coated.

3. Let the salad sit at room temperature for about 30 minutes before serving, giving it another toss just before serving. Enjoy!

Nutrition: Calories 243, Fat 19.4 g, Protein 11.11 g, Carbohydrates 7.31 g, Sugar 1.66 g, Fiber 0.7 g

35. Avocado Gazpacho

Prep Time: 15 minutes

Cook Time: 0-minute

Serving: 4

Ingredients

- 2 cups chopped tomatoes
- 2 large ripe avocados
- 1 large cucumber
- 1 medium bell pepper
- 1 cup plain whole-milk Greek yogurt
- ¼ cup extra-virgin olive oil
- ¼ cup chopped fresh cilantro
- ¼ cup chopped scallions
- 2 tablespoons red wine vinegar
- Juice of 2 limes or 1 lemon
- ½ to 1 teaspoon salt
- ¼ teaspoon black pepper

Directions

1. In a blender or large bowl (if using an immersion blender), combine the chopped tomatoes, avocados, cucumber, bell pepper, Greek yogurt, olive oil, cilantro, scallions, red wine vinegar, and lime juice. Blend until the mixture becomes smooth.

2. Add salt and black pepper to taste, and blend again to combine the flavours.

3. Refrigerate the gazpacho for at least 2 hours before serving so it becomes chilled and the flavours meld together.

4. Serve the cold gazpacho and enjoy!

Nutrition: Calories 286, Fat 22.8 g, Protein 5.73 g, Carbohydrates 19.38 g, Sugar 7.54 g, Fiber 8.6 g

36. Roasted Garlic Hummus

Prep Time: 9 minutes

Cook Time: 33 minutes

Serving: 4

Ingredients

- 1 cup dried chickpeas
- 4 cups water
- 1 tablespoon plus ¼ cup extra-virgin olive oil, divided
- 1/3 cup tahini
- 1 teaspoon ground cumin
- ½ teaspoon onion powder
- ¾ teaspoon salt
- ½ teaspoon ground black pepper
- 1/3 cup lemon juice
- 3 tablespoons mashed roasted garlic
- 2 tablespoons chopped fresh parsley

Directions

1. Add the dried chickpeas, water, and 1 tablespoon of olive oil to an Instant Pot®. Cover and set the Manual button to 30 minutes. Once the timer beeps, quick-release the pressure and select the Cancel button to open. Drain the chickpeas, reserving the cooking liquid.

2. In a food processor, combine the chickpeas, ¼ cup of olive oil, tahini, cumin, onion powder, salt, pepper, lemon juice, and roasted garlic. Process the ingredients until smooth.

3. Transfer the hummus to a bowl and top with chopped parsley. Serve at room temperature.

Note: If you prefer a thinner consistency, add some of the reserved cooking liquid to the hummus and blend again until the desired consistency is reached.

Nutrition: Calories 699, Fat 45.7 g, Protein 34.63 g, Carbohydrates 40.1 g, Sugar 6.34 g, Fiber 8.3 g

37. Red Pepper Hummus

Prep Time: 7 minutes
Cook Time: 34 minutes
Serving: 4

Ingredients

- 1 cup dried chickpeas
- 4 cups water
- 1 tablespoon plus ¼ cup extra-virgin olive oil, divided
- ½ cup chopped roasted red pepper, divided
- 1/3 cup tahini
- 1 teaspoon ground cumin
- ¾ teaspoon salt
- ½ teaspoon ground black pepper
- ¼ teaspoon smoked paprika
- 1/3 cup lemon juice
- ½ teaspoon minced garlic

Directions

1. In an Instant Pot®, combine the dried chickpeas, water, and 1 tablespoon of olive oil. Seal the Instant Pot® and set the steam release to "Sealing." Select the "Manual" button and set the timer for 30 minutes.

2. Once the timer goes off, quick-release the pressure and select the "Cancel" button to open the Instant Pot®. Drain the chickpeas, reserving the cooking liquid.

3. In a food processor, combine the chickpeas, 1/3 cup of roasted red pepper, tahini, cumin, salt, black pepper,

smoked paprika, lemon juice, minced garlic, and the remaining 1/4 cup of olive oil. Process until smooth.

4. Garnish the hummus with the reserved roasted red pepper and serve. This recipe is a great addition to a Mediterranean diet. Enjoy!

Nutrition: Calories 275, Fat 24.2 g, Protein 3.3 g, Carbohydrates 12.02 g, Sugar 3.08 g, Fiber 2.8 g

38. White Bean Hummus

Prep Time: 11 minutes
Cook Time: 40 minutes
Serving: 12

Ingredients

- 2/3 cup dried white beans
- 3 cloves garlic, peeled and crushed
- ¼ cup olive oil
- 1 tablespoon lemon juice
- ½ teaspoon salt

Directions

1. Place the dried white beans and crushed garlic in the Instant Pot® and stir to combine. Add enough cold water to cover the ingredients, then cover the pot and set the steam release valve to "Sealing". Use the Manual button to set the cooking time to 30 minutes.

2. Once the cooking time is up, allow the pressure to naturally release for 20 minutes. Then, cancel the cooking cycle and open the lid. Check that the beans are tender using a fork, and drain off any excess water.

3. Transfer the cooked beans and garlic to a food processor. Add the olive oil, lemon juice, and salt, and pulse the mixture until it is mostly smooth with some small chunks remaining.

4. Transfer the white bean hummus to a container and refrigerate for at least 4 hours. Serve cold or at room temperature as desired.

Nutrition: Calories 79, Fat 4.6 g, Protein 2.6 g, Carbohydrates 7.13 g, Sugar 0.28 g, Fiber 1.7 g

39. Kidney Bean Dip with Cilantro, Cumin, and Lime

Prep Time: 13 minutes
Cook Time: 51 minutes
Serving: 16

Ingredients

- 1 cup dried kidney beans
- 4 cups water
- 3 cloves garlic
- ¼ cup cilantro
- ¼ cup extra-virgin olive oil
- 1 tablespoon lime juice
- 2 teaspoons grated lime zest
- 1 teaspoon ground cumin
- ½ teaspoon salt

Directions

1. In the Instant Pot®, combine the kidney beans, water, garlic, and 2 tablespoons of cilantro. Close the lid, set the steam release to Sealing, and press the Bean button. Cook for 30 minutes.

2. When the timer goes off, allow the pressure to naturally release for about 20 minutes. Press the Cancel button, open the lid, and check that the beans are tender. Drain any excess water and transfer the beans to a medium bowl. Using a potato masher, gently mash the beans.

3. Add the olive oil, lime juice, zest, cumin, salt, and the remaining 2 tablespoons of cilantro to the bowl and stir to combine. Serve warm or at room temperature.

Nutrition: Calories 22, Fat 1.96 g, Protein 0.35 g, Carbohydrates 0.81 g, Sugar 0.04 g, Fiber 0.1 g

40. White Bean Dip with Garlic and Herbs

Prep Time: 10 minutes

Cook Time: 48 minutes

Serving: 16

Ingredients

- 1 cup dried white beans
- 3 cloves garlic
- 8 cups water
- ¼ cup extra-virgin olive oil
- ¼ cup chopped fresh flat-leaf parsley
- 1 tablespoon fresh oregano
- 1 tablespoon d fresh tarragon
- 1 teaspoon fresh thyme leaves
- 1 teaspoon lemon zest
- ¼ teaspoon salt
- ¼ teaspoon black pepper
- 2 small jalapeño peppers
- 1 small onion
- ½ cup chopped fresh cilantro
- 1 teaspoon ground coriander
- 1 teaspoon sea salt
- 1½ cups water

Directions

1. Add the dried white beans and garlic to the Instant Pot® and mix well. Pour 8 cups of water, close the lid, set the steam release to Sealing, and select the Manual button. Adjust the time to 30 minutes and let it cook.

2. Once the timer beeps, naturally release the pressure for about 20 minutes. Then, open the lid and check if the beans are soft. Press the Cancel button, drain off any excess

water, and transfer the beans and garlic to a food processor along with the olive oil.

3. Add the parsley, oregano, tarragon, thyme, lemon zest, salt, and black pepper to the food processor and pulse 3-5 times to combine everything. Chill the mixture in the refrigerator for at least 4 hours or overnight. Serve the white bean dip cold or at room temperature.

Nutrition: Calories 62, Fat 1.6 g, Protein 3.3 g, Carbohydrates 9.01 g, Sugar 0.81 g, Fiber 2.2 g

Snack Recipes

41. Cucumber Sandwich Bites

Prep Time: 5 minutes

Cook Time: 0 minute

Serving: 12

Ingredients

- 1 cucumber, sliced
- 8 slices whole wheat bread
- 2 tablespoons cream cheese, soft
- 1 tablespoon chives, chopped
- ¼ cup avocado, peeled, pitted, and mashed
- 1 teaspoon mustard
- Salt and black pepper to the taste

Directions

1. Cut the cucumber into thin slices.

2. In a small bowl, mix the cream cheese, chopped chives, mashed avocado, and mustard.

3. Season with salt and black pepper to taste.

4. Spread the avocado mixture on each slice of whole wheat bread.

5. Place the cucumber slices on half the bread slices, then top with the other bread slices to make sandwiches.

6. Cut each sandwich into thirds to make bite-sized pieces.

7. Arrange the cucumber sandwich bites on a platter and serve them as appetizers.

Nutrition: Calories 68, Fat 1.97 g, Protein 3 g, Carbohydrates 9.87 g, Sugar 1.24 g, Fiber 1.6 g

42. Yogurt Dip

Prep Time: 10 minutes

Cook Time: 0 minute

Serving: 6

Ingredients

- 2 cups Greek yogurt
- 2 tablespoons pistachios, toasted and chopped
- A pinch of salt and white pepper
- 2 tablespoons mint, chopped
- 1 tablespoon kalamata olives, pitted and chopped
- ¼ cup zaatar spice
- ¼ cup pomegranate seeds
- 1/3 cup olive oil

Directions

1. In a bowl, mix the Greek yogurt, toasted and chopped pistachios, salt, white pepper, chopped mint, kalamata olives, zaatar spice, and pomegranate seeds.

2. Whisk the ingredients well to combine.

3. Divide the mixture into small cups.

4. Drizzle olive oil on top of the dip.

5. Serve the dip with pita chips on the side.

Nutrition: Calories 273, Fat 19.3 g, Protein 20 g, Carbohydrates 4.9 g, Sugar 3.41 g, Fiber 0.7 g

43. Tomato Bruschetta

Prep Time: 10 minutes

Cook Time: 10 minutes

Serving: 6

Ingredients

- 1 baguette, sliced
- 1/3 cup basil, chopped
- 6 tomatoes, cubed
- 2 garlic cloves, minced
- A pinch of salt and black pepper
- 1 teaspoon olive oil
- 1 tablespoon balsamic vinegar
- ½ teaspoon garlic powder
- Cooking spray

Directions

1. Preheat your oven to 400 degrees F (200 degrees C) and line a baking sheet with parchment paper.

2. Arrange the baguette slices on the prepared baking sheet and lightly spray them with cooking spray.

3. Bake the baguette slices for about 10 minutes or until lightly toasted.

4. In a mixing bowl, combine the cubed tomatoes, chopped basil, minced garlic, olive oil, balsamic vinegar, garlic powder, salt, and black pepper. Toss well to combine, and let the mixture sit for 10 minutes to allow the flavors to meld together.

5. Divide the tomato mixture evenly over the toasted baguette slices.

6. Arrange the bruschetta on a serving platter and serve immediately.

Nutrition: Calories 270, Fat 21 g, Protein 13.8 g, Carbohydrates 6.5 g, Sugar 4.04 g, Fiber 1.7 g

44. Olives and Cheese Stuffed Tomatoes

Prep Time: 10 minutes

Cook Time: 0 minute

Serving: 24

Ingredients

- 24 cherry tomatoes, top cut off and insides scooped out
- 2 tablespoons olive oil
- ¼ teaspoon red pepper flakes
- ½ cup feta cheese, crumbled
- 2 tablespoons black olive paste
- ¼ cup mint, torn

Directions

1. In a mixing bowl, combine the black olive paste with the rest of the ingredients except for the cherry tomatoes, and whisk everything together well.

2. Stuff the cherry tomatoes with the mixture using a spoon or a piping bag.

3. Arrange the stuffed tomatoes on a platter and serve them as an appetizer.

Nutrition: Calories 24, Fat 1.9 g, Protein 0.6 g, Carbohydrates 1.2 g, Sugar 0.89 g, Fiber 0.2 g

45. Pepper Tapenade

Prep Time: 10 minutes

Cook Time: 0 minute

Serving: 4

Ingredients

- 7 ounces roasted red peppers, chopped
- ½ cup parmesan, grated
- 1/3 cup parsley, chopped
- 14 ounces canned artichokes, drained and chopped
- 3 tablespoons olive oil
- ¼ cup capers, drained
- 1 and ½ tablespoons lemon juice
- 2 garlic cloves, minced

Directions

1. Add the roasted red peppers, grated parmesan, chopped parsley, canned artichokes, olive oil, drained capers, lemon juice, and minced garlic into a blender.

2. Pulse the ingredients until they are well combined and form a smooth paste.

3. Divide the pepper tapenade into cups and serve as a snack.

Nutrition: Calories 197, Fat 11.12 g, Protein 7.59 g, Carbohydrates 19.99 g, Sugar 3.47 g, Fiber 9.4 g

46. Coriander Falafel

Prep Time: 10 minutes

Cook Time: 10 minutes

Serving: 8

Ingredients

- 1 cup canned garbanzo beans
- 1 bunch parsley leaves
- 1 yellow onion, chopped
- 5 garlic cloves, minced
- 1 teaspoon coriander, ground
- A pinch of salt and black pepper
- ¼ teaspoon cayenne pepper
- ¼ teaspoon baking soda
- ¼ teaspoon cumin powder
- 1 teaspoon lemon juice
- 3 tablespoons tapioca flour
- Olive oil for frying

Directions

1. In a food processor, combine the garbanzo beans, parsley, onion, garlic, coriander, salt, black pepper, cayenne pepper, baking soda, cumin powder, and lemon juice. Pulse until well mixed.

2. Transfer the mixture to a bowl, add the tapioca flour, and stir well to combine. Shape the mixture into 16 balls and slightly flatten them.

3. Heat olive oil in a pan over medium-high heat. Add the falafel balls and cook for 5 minutes on each side until golden brown and crispy. Drain excess grease on paper towels.

4. Arrange the falafel on a platter and serve it as an appetizer.

Nutrition: Calories 117, Fat 2.78 g, Protein 5.68 g, Carbohydrates 18.2 g, Sugar 3.53 g, Fiber 3.6 g

47. Chickpeas and Red Pepper Hummus

Prep Time: 10 minutes

Cook Time: 0 minute

Serving: 6

Ingredients

- 6 ounces roasted red peppers, peeled and chopped
- 16 ounces canned chickpeas, drained and rinsed
- ¼ cup Greek yogurt
- 3 tablespoons tahini paste
- Juice of 1 lemon
- 3 garlic cloves, minced
- 1 tablespoon olive oil
- A pinch of salt and black pepper
- 1 tablespoon parsley, chopped

Directions

1. Add the roasted red peppers, chickpeas, Greek yogurt, tahini paste, lemon juice, minced garlic, salt, and black pepper to a food processor. Pulse the ingredients until they are smooth and well combined.

2. Drizzle in the olive oil while continuing to pulse until the oil is fully incorporated.

3. Transfer the hummus to a serving dish or individual cups, sprinkle chopped parsley on top, and serve. This makes a great party spread or dip.

Nutrition: Calories 188, Fat 8.28 g, Protein 7.87 g, Carbohydrates 22.6 g, Sugar 5.14 g, Fiber 6 g

48. White Bean Dip

Prep Time: 10 minutes

Cook Time: 0 minute

Serving: 4

Ingredients

- 15 ounces canned white beans, drained and rinsed
- 6 ounces canned artichoke hearts, drained and quartered
- 4 garlic cloves, minced
- 1 tablespoon basil, chopped
- 2 tablespoons olive oil
- Juice of ½ lemon
- Zest of ½ lemon, grated
- Salt and black pepper to the taste

Directions

1. Add the canned white beans, canned artichoke hearts, minced garlic, chopped basil, lemon juice, grated lemon zest, salt, and black pepper to a food processor. Pulse the mixture until well combined.

2. Gradually add the olive oil while pulsing the mixture again.

3. Transfer the dip into cups or a bowl, and serve as a party dip.

Nutrition: Calories 309, Fat 11.32 g, Protein 23.11 g, Carbohydrates 29.58 g, Sugar 1.27 g, Fiber 7 g

49. Hummus with Ground Lamb

Prep Time: 10 minutes

Cook Time: 15 minutes

Serving: 8

Ingredients

- 10 ounces hummus
- 12 ounces lamb meat, ground
- ½ cup pomegranate seeds
- ¼ cup parsley, chopped
- 1 tablespoon olive oil
- Pita chips for serving

Directions

1. Heat a pan over medium-high heat. Add the ground lamb and cook for about 15 minutes, often stirring, until browned.

2. Spread the hummus on a platter, and then spread the cooked lamb all over it.

3. Sprinkle the pomegranate seeds and chopped parsley on top.

4. Serve the hummus and lamb mixture with pita chips as a snack.

Nutrition: Calories 145, Fat 7.37 g, Protein 9.08 g, Carbohydrates 10.63 g, Sugar 2.52 g, Fiber 2.2 g

50. Veggie Fritters

Prep Time: 10 minutes

Cook Time: 10 minutes

Serving: 8

Ingredients

- 2 garlic cloves, minced
- 2 yellow onions, chopped
- 4 scallions, chopped
- 2 carrots, grated
- 2 teaspoons cumin, ground
- ½ teaspoon turmeric powder
- Salt and black pepper to the taste
- ¼ teaspoon coriander, ground
- 2 tablespoons parsley, chopped
- ¼ teaspoon lemon juice
- ½ cup almond flour
- 2 beets, peeled and grated
- 2 eggs, whisked
- ¼ cup tapioca flour
- 3 tablespoons olive oil

Directions

1. In a mixing bowl, combine minced garlic, chopped yellow onions, chopped scallions, grated carrots, ground cumin, turmeric powder, coriander, chopped parsley, lemon juice, almond flour, grated beets, whisked eggs, tapioca flour, salt, and black pepper. Mix well to form a batter for fritters.

2. Heat 3 tablespoons of olive oil in a frying pan over medium-high heat.

3. Using a spoon, shape the batter into medium-sized fritters and gently place them in the hot oil.

4. Cook for about 5 minutes on each side until the fritters are golden brown.

5. Once done, remove the fritters from the pan and transfer them to a plate lined with paper towels to remove excess oil.

6. Arrange the fritters on a platter and serve them hot.

Nutrition: Calories 147, Fat 10.09 g, Protein 3.38 g, Carbohydrates 11.3 g, Sugar 3.89 g, Fiber 1.8 g

51. Bulgur Lamb Meatballs

Prep Time: 10 minutes

Cook Time: 15 minutes

Serving: 6

Ingredients

- 1 and ½ cups Greek yogurt
- ½ teaspoon cumin, ground
- 1 cup cucumber, shredded
- ½ teaspoon garlic, minced
- A pinch of salt and black pepper
- 1 cup bulgur
- 2 cups water
- 1-pound lamb, ground
- ¼ cup parsley, chopped
- ¼ cup shallots, chopped
- ½ teaspoon allspice, ground
- ½ teaspoon cinnamon powder
- 1 tablespoon olive oil

Directions

1. In a bowl, mix the bulgur with water, cover it, and let it sit for 10 minutes. Drain any excess water and transfer the bulgur to another bowl.

2. Add the ground lamb, yogurt, parsley, shallots, allspice, cinnamon powder, garlic, cumin, salt, and black pepper to the bowl with bulgur. Mix everything well until evenly combined.

3. Using your hands, shape the mixture into medium-sized meatballs.

4. Heat a pan over medium-high heat and add olive oil. Once hot, add the meatballs to the pan, and cook for about 7 minutes on each side or until browned and cooked through.

5. Arrange the meatballs on a platter and serve them as an appetizer.

Nutrition: Calories 266, Fat 15.2 g, Protein 22.8 g, Carbohydrates 8.89 g, Sugar 1.89 g, Fiber 2 g

52. Cucumber Bites

Prep Time: 10 minutes

Cook Time: 0 minute

Serving: 12

Ingredients

- 1 English cucumber, sliced into 32 rounds
- 10 ounces hummus
- 16 cherry tomatoes, halved
- 1 tablespoon parsley, chopped
- 1-ounce feta cheese, crumbled

Directions

1. Arrange the cucumber rounds on a platter.

2. Spread 1 teaspoon of hummus on top of each cucumber round.

3. Place half a cherry tomato on top of each hummus-covered cucumber round.

4. Sprinkle crumbled feta cheese and chopped parsley over the tomato halves.

5. Serve immediately as an appetizer.

Nutrition: Calories 55, Fat 2.56 g, Protein 1.61 g, Carbohydrates 6.63 g, Sugar 1.57 g, Fiber 1.2 g

53. Stuffed Avocado

Prep Time: 10 minutes

Cook Time: 0 minute

Serving: 2

Ingredients

- 1 avocado, halved and pitted
- 10 ounces canned tuna, drained
- 2 tablespoons sun-dried tomatoes, chopped
- 1 and ½ tablespoon basil pesto
- 2 tablespoons black olives, pitted and chopped
- Salt and black pepper to the taste
- 2 teaspoons pine nuts, toasted and chopped
- 1 tablespoon basil, chopped

Directions

1. Mix the tuna, sun-dried tomatoes, and all other ingredients except the avocado.

2. Thoroughly stir the mixture. Then, take the avocado halves and fill them with the tuna mixture.

3. Serve the stuffed avocado halves as an appetizer.

Nutrition: Calories 324, Fat 18.55 g, Protein 31 g, Carbohydrates 13.28 g, Sugar 3.2 g, Fiber 7.8 g

54. Wrapped Plums

Prep Time: 5 minutes

Cook Time: 0 minute

Serving: 8

Ingredients

- 2 ounces prosciutto, cut into 16 pieces

- 4 plums, quartered

- 1 tablespoon chives, chopped

- A pinch of red pepper flakes, crushed

Directions

1. Quarter 4 plums.

2. Cut 2 ounces of prosciutto into 16 pieces, and then wrap each plum quarter with a slice of prosciutto.

3. Arrange the wrapped plums on a platter, then sprinkle chopped chives and crushed red pepper flakes over the top. Serve the dish immediately.

Note: This appetizer recipe takes only 5 minutes to prepare and doesn't require any cooking.

Nutrition: Calories 35, Fat 0.81 g, Protein 1.57 g, Carbohydrates 5.94 g, Sugar 5.4 g, Fiber 0.3 g

55. Spiced Salmon Crudités

Prep Time: 10 minutes

Cook Time: 15 minutes

Serving: 4

Ingredients

- 6 ounces smoked wild salmon

- 2 tablespoons Roasted Garlic Aioli

- 1 tablespoon Dijon mustard

- 1 tablespoon chopped scallions, green parts only

- 2 teaspoons chopped capers

- ½ teaspoon dried dill

- 4 endive spears or hearts of romaine

- ½ English cucumber, cut into ¼-inch-thick rounds

Directions

1. Roughly chop the smoked wild salmon and place it into a small bowl.

2. Add the Roasted Garlic Aioli, Dijon mustard, chopped scallions (green parts only), chopped capers, and dried dill to the bowl. Mix well to combine all the ingredients.

3. Arrange the endive spears or hearts of romaine and cucumber rounds on a platter or individual serving plates.

4. Spoon a generous amount of the smoked salmon mixture onto each endive spear and cucumber round, evenly spreading it.

5. Serve the Spiced Salmon Crudités chilled and enjoy as a healthy and flavorful appetizer or snack.

Nutrition: Calories 179, Fat 4.76 g, Protein 17.9 g, Carbohydrates 19.8 g, Sugar 1.78 g, Fiber 16.5 g

56. All-Spiced Olives

Prep Time: 4 hours and 10 minutes

Cook Time: 0 minute

Serving: 2

Ingredients

- 2 cups mixed green olives with pits
- ¼ cup red wine vinegar
- ¼ cup extra-virgin olive oil
- 4 garlic cloves, finely minced
- Zest and juice of 1 large orange
- 1 teaspoon red pepper flakes
- 2 bay leaves
- ½ teaspoon ground cumin
- ½ teaspoon ground allspice

Directions

1. In a bowl, combine the mixed green olives with pits, red wine vinegar, extra-virgin olive oil, finely minced garlic, orange zest and juice, red pepper flakes, bay leaves, ground cumin, and ground allspice. Mix well to ensure all the olives are coated with the marinade.

2. Cover the bowl and place it in the refrigerator for at least 4 hours, or up to a week, to allow the olives to marinate. Toss the olives again before serving to evenly distribute the marinade.

3. Serve the all-spiced olives chilled as a flavorful and healthy snack or appetizer.

Nutrition: Calories 216, Fat 12.39 g, Protein 5.7 g, Carbohydrates 23.8 g, Sugar 9.8 g, Fiber 7.1 g

57. Pitted Olives and Anchovies

Prep Time: 1 hour and 10 minutes

Cook Time: 0 minute

Serving: 2

Ingredients

- 2 cups pitted Kalamata olives or other black olives
- 2 anchovy fillets, chopped
- 2 teaspoons chopped capers
- 1 garlic clove, finely minced
- 1 cooked egg yolk
- 1 teaspoon Dijon mustard
- ¼ cup extra-virgin olive oil
- Seedy Crackers, Versatile Sandwich Round, or vegetables, for serving (optional)

Directions

1. Wash the olives in cold water and strain them well.

2. In a food processor, blender, or a large jar if using an immersion blender, combine the olives, chopped anchovies, capers, minced garlic, cooked egg yolk, and Dijon mustard.

3. Process the mixture until it forms a thick paste, gradually streaming in the olive oil while running.

4. Transfer the mixture to a small bowl, cover it, and refrigerate for at least one hour to allow the flavors to develop.

5. Serve the pitted olives and anchovies with seedy crackers, a versatile sandwich round, or your favorite crunchy vegetables.

Nutrition: Calories 309, Fat 29.19 g, Protein 4.24 g, Carbohydrates 10.76 g, Sugar 0.25 g, Fiber 4.7 g

58. Medi Deviled Eggs

Prep Time: 45 minutes

Cook Time: 15 minutes

Serving: 4

Ingredients

- 4 large hardboiled eggs
- 2 tablespoons Roasted Garlic Aioli
- ½ cup finely crumbled feta cheese
- 8 pitted Kalamata olives, finely chopped
- 2 tablespoons chopped sun-dried tomatoes
- 1 tablespoon minced red onion
- ½ teaspoon dried dill
- ¼ teaspoon freshly ground black pepper

Directions

1. Cut the hardboiled eggs in half lengthwise, and remove the yolks, placing them in a medium bowl. Set the egg white halves aside. Use a fork to smash the yolks well, then add the Roasted Garlic Aioli, crumbled feta, chopped olives, sun-dried tomatoes, minced red onion, dried dill, and black pepper, stirring well to combine until the mixture is smooth and creamy.

2. Spoon the filling into each egg white half and refrigerate for at least 30 minutes, or up to 24 hours, covered, to allow the flavors to meld.

Nutrition: Calories 121, Fat 9.09 g, Protein 6.09 g, Carbohydrates 4.01 g, Sugar 1.27 g, Fiber 0.6 g

59. Cheese Crackers

Prep Time: 1 hour and 15 minutes

Cook Time: 15 minutes

Serving: 20

Ingredients

- 4 tablespoons butter, at room temperature
- 1 cup finely shredded Manchego cheese
- 1 cup almond flour
- 1 teaspoon salt, divided
- ¼ teaspoon freshly ground black pepper
- 1 large egg

Directions

1. Using an electric mixer, beat the butter and shredded cheese until smooth. Add the almond flour, ½-teaspoon salt, and pepper. Gradually mix in the almond flour mixture until the dough forms a ball.

2. Place the dough on a piece of parchment or plastic wrap and roll it into a cylinder log about 1½ inches thick. Seal tightly and freeze for at least 1 hour. Preheat the oven to 350°F and line 2 baking sheets with parchment paper or silicone baking mats.

3. To make the egg wash, beat the egg and the remaining ½-teaspoon salt. Slice the refrigerated dough into small rounds, about ¼ inch thick, and place them on the prepared baking sheets.

4. Brush the tops of the crackers with the egg wash and bake until they are golden and crispy. Transfer the crackers to a wire rack to cool.

5. Serve the crackers warm or store them in an airtight container in the refrigerator for up to 1 week.

Nutrition: Calories 42, Fat 4.01 g, Protein 1.28 g, Carbohydrates 0.23 g, Sugar 0.15 g, Fiber 0 g

60. Cheesy Caprese Stack

Prep Time: 5 minutes

Cook Time: 0 minute

Serving: 4

Ingredients

- 1 large organic tomato, preferably heirloom
- ½ teaspoon salt
- ¼ teaspoon freshly ground black pepper
- 1 (4-ounce) ball burrata cheese
- 8 fresh basil leaves, thinly sliced
- 2 tablespoons extra-virgin olive oil
- 1 tablespoon red wine or balsamic vinegar

Directions

1. Cut the tomato into 4 thick slices, remove the core, and sprinkle them with salt and pepper. Place the seasoned tomato slices on a plate.

2. Slice the burrata into 4 thick slices, and place one slice on top of each tomato slice on a separate plate.

3. Add one-quarter of the sliced basil on top of each burrata and pour any reserved cream from the burrata over the top.

4. Drizzle with olive oil and vinegar.

5. Serve the Cheesy Caprese Stack with a fork and knife.

Nutrition: Calories 121, Fat 9.86 g, Protein 5.61 g, Carbohydrates 2.76 g, Sugar 1.86 g, Fiber 0.6 g

Dinner Recipes

61. Crispy Mediterranean Chicken Thighs

Prep Time: 9 minutes

Cook Time: 35 minutes

Serving: 6

Ingredients

- 2 tablespoons extra-virgin olive oil
- 2 teaspoons dried rosemary
- 1½ teaspoons ground cumin
- 1½ teaspoons ground coriander
- ¾ teaspoon dried oregano
- 1/8 teaspoon salt
- 6 chicken thighs (about 3 pounds)

Directions

1. Preheat your oven to 450°F and line a baking sheet with parchment paper.

2. In a large bowl, mix 2 tablespoons of extra-virgin olive oil, 2 teaspoons of dried rosemary, 1½ teaspoons of ground cumin, 1½ teaspoons of ground coriander, ¾ teaspoon of dried oregano, and 1/8 teaspoon of salt, forming a paste.

3. Add 6 chicken thighs (about 3 pounds) to the bowl and mix until evenly coated with the spice paste.

4. Place the chicken on the prepared baking sheet.

5. Bake for 30 to 35 minutes.

6. Remove from the oven, let cool for a few minutes, and serve.

7. Enjoy your Crispy Mediterranean Chicken Thighs!

Nutrition: Calories 477, Fat 34.02 g, Protein 32.02 g, Carbohydrates 0.86 g, Sugar 0.02 g, Fiber 0.1 g

62. Greek Penne and Chicken

Prep Time: 11 minutes

Cook Time: 9 minutes

Serving: 4

Ingredients

- 16-ounce package of Penne Pasta
- 1-pound Chicken Breast Halves
- 1/2 cup of Chopped Red Onion
- 1 1/2 tablespoons of Butter
- 2 cloves of Minced Garlic
- 14-ounce can of Artichoke Hearts
- 1 Chopped Tomato
- 3 tablespoons of Chopped Fresh Parsley
- 1/2 cup of Crumbled Feta Cheese
- 2 tablespoons of Lemon Juice
- 1 teaspoon of Dried Oregano
- Ground Black Pepper
- Salt

Directions

1. Melt butter in a large skillet over medium-high heat. Add minced garlic and chopped red onion, and cook for about 2 minutes. Add chicken breast halves and cook until golden brown, occasionally stirring, for about 5-6 minutes.

2. Reduce heat to medium-low. Drain and chop artichoke hearts, and add them to the skillet with chopped tomato,

fresh parsley, crumbled feta cheese, dried oregano, lemon juice, and cooked penne pasta. Cook for 2-3 minutes, occasionally stirring.

3. Season with ground black pepper and salt to taste. Serve and enjoy!

Nutrition: Calories 394, Fat 10.01 g, Protein 29.57 g, Carbohydrates 50.12 g, Sugar 3.45 g, Fiber 11.7 g

63. Yogurt-Marinated Chicken Kebabs

Prep Time: 31 minutes

Cook Time: 20 minutes

Serving: 4

Ingredients

- ½ cup plain Greek yogurt
- 1 tablespoon lemon juice
- ½ teaspoon ground cumin
- ½ teaspoon ground coriander
- ½ teaspoon kosher salt
- ¼ teaspoon cayenne pepper
- 1½ pound chicken breast

Directions

1. In a large bowl, whisk together the Greek yogurt, lemon juice, cumin, coriander, salt, and cayenne pepper until smooth. Add the chicken breast and toss to coat evenly. Cover the bowl with plastic wrap and marinate in the refrigerator for at least 30 minutes or overnight.

2. Preheat the grill to medium-high heat. Thread the chicken pieces onto skewers, discarding the marinade. Grill the kebabs for 18-20 minutes, occasionally turning, until the chicken is cooked through and browned on all sides.

3. Remove the kebabs from the grill and let them rest for 5 minutes before serving. Enjoy!

Note: You can also bake the kebabs in the oven instead of grilling them. Preheat the oven to 425°F and line a baking sheet with parchment paper. Place the chicken skewers on the baking sheet and bake for 20-25 minutes or until the chicken is cooked through.

Nutrition: Calories 307, Fat 15.9 g, Protein 37 g, Carbohydrates 1.22 g, Sugar 0.8 g, Fiber 0.1 g

64. Braised Chicken with Roasted Bell Peppers

Prep Time: 7 minutes

Cook Time: 54 minutes

Serving: 8

Ingredients

- 2 tablespoons extra-virgin olive oil
- 4 pounds bone-in chicken, breast and thighs, skin removed
- 1½ teaspoon kosher salt, divided
- ¼ teaspoon freshly ground black pepper
- 1 onion, julienned
- 6 garlic cloves, sliced
- 1 cup white wine
- 2 pounds tomatoes, chopped
- ¼ teaspoon red pepper flakes
- 3 bell peppers
- 1/3 cup fresh parsley, chopped
- 1 tablespoon lemon juice

Directions

1. Heat olive oil in a large Dutch oven or skillet over medium-high heat. Season chicken with ¾-teaspoon salt and black pepper. Brown half of the chicken on each side for about 2 minutes and then transfer to a plate. Repeat with remaining chicken.

2. Lower the heat to medium and add onion. Sauté for about 5 minutes, add garlic, and sauté for another 30 seconds. Pour

in the wine, increase heat to medium-high, and boil to deglaze the skillet. Reduce the liquid for 6 minutes. Mix in tomatoes, red pepper flakes, and the remaining ¾-teaspoon salt. Add chicken back to the skillet, cover, reduce heat to low, and simmer for 40 minutes, rotating the chicken halfway through the cooking time.

3. While the chicken is cooking, roast the bell peppers. If using raw peppers, refer to the roasting method. If using jarred peppers, skip to step 4.

4. Chop the bell peppers into 1-inch pieces and set aside.

5. Transfer the cooked chicken to a plate.

6. Increase the heat to high and bring the mixture to a boil. Reduce by half, about 10 minutes.

7. Debone the chicken once cool enough and return it to the skillet with the bell peppers.

8. Simmer for 5 minutes to heat through. Stir in parsley and lemon juice.

Nutrition: Calories 546, Fat 12.9 g, Protein 83 g, Carbohydrates 29.1 g, Sugar 7.25 g, Fiber 3.3 g

65. Chicken Stew with Artichokes, Capers, and Olives

Prep Time: 6 minutes

Cook Time: 33 minutes

Serving: 4

Ingredients

- 1½ pounds boneless, skinless chicken thighs
- 1 teaspoon kosher salt, divided
- ¼ teaspoon freshly ground black pepper
- 2 tablespoons olive oil
- 1 onion, julienned
- 4 garlic cloves, sliced
- 1 teaspoon ground turmeric
- 1 teaspoon ground cumin
- ½ teaspoon ground coriander
- ½ teaspoon ground cinnamon
- ¼ teaspoon red pepper flakes
- 1 dried bay leaf
- 1¼ cups no-salt-added chicken stock
- ¼ cup white wine vinegar
- 2 tablespoons lemon juice
- 1 tablespoon lemon zest
- 1 (14-ounce) can artichoke hearts, drained
- ¼ cup olives, pitted and chopped
- 1 teaspoon capers, rinsed and chopped

- 1 tablespoon fresh mint, chopped

- 1 tablespoon fresh parsley, chopped

Directions

1. Season the chicken with 1/2 teaspoon of salt and pepper.

2. Heat olive oil in a large skillet over medium heat. Cook the chicken for 3 minutes per side, then transfer to a plate and set aside.

3. In the same pan, sauté the onion until translucent, about 5 minutes. Add the garlic and sauté for another 30 seconds. Add the remaining 1/2 teaspoon of salt, turmeric, cumin, coriander, cinnamon, red pepper flakes, and bay leaf, and sauté for 30 seconds.

4. Add 1/4 cup of the chicken stock to deglaze the pan, and increase the heat to medium high. Then, add the remaining 1 cup of stock, lemon juice, and lemon zest. Cover, set the heat to low, and simmer for 10 minutes.

5. Add the artichokes, olives, and capers, and mix well. Add the reserved chicken and nestle it into the mixture. Simmer for 15 minutes. Garnish with the mint and parsley before serving.

Nutrition: Calories 502, Fat 22.2 g, Protein 28.15 g, Carbohydrates 47 g, Sugar 11 g, Fiber 7.5 g

66. Zaatar Chicken Tenders

Prep Time: 8 minutes

Cook Time: 15 minutes

Serving: 4

Ingredients

- Olive oil cooking spray
- 1-pound chicken tenders
- 1½ tablespoons zaatar
- ½ teaspoon kosher salt
- ¼ teaspoon freshly ground black pepper

Directions

1. Preheat your oven to 400°F and line a baking sheet with parchment paper. Spray the parchment paper with olive oil cooking spray.

2. In a large bowl, combine the chicken tenders with the zaatar, kosher salt, and black pepper. Mix well until the chicken tenders are fully coated with the spices.

3. Arrange the chicken tenders in a single layer on the prepared baking sheet.

4. Place the baking sheet in the oven and bake for 15 minutes, turning the chicken tenders over once halfway through the cooking time.

5. Once done, remove from the oven and serve immediately. Enjoy!

Nutrition: Calories 286, Fat 14.6 g, Protein 18.5 g, Carbohydrates 20 g, Sugar 0 g, Fiber 0 g

67. Lemon Chicken with Artichokes and Crispy Kale

Prep Time: 9 minutes

Cook Time: 35 minutes

Serving: 4

Ingredients

- 3 tablespoons extra-virgin olive oil, divided
- 2 tablespoons lemon juice
- Zest of 1 lemon
- 2 garlic cloves, minced
- 2 teaspoons dried rosemary
- ¼ teaspoon freshly ground black pepper
- 1½ pounds boneless, skinless chicken breast
- 2 (14-ounce) cans artichoke hearts, drained
- 1 bunch (about 6 ounces) Lacinato kale

Directions

1. In a bowl, combine 2 tablespoons of olive oil, lemon juice, lemon zest, garlic, rosemary, salt, and black pepper. Mix well and add chicken and artichokes. Marinate in the fridge for at least 30 minutes and up to 4 hours.

2. Remove chicken and artichokes from the marinade and arrange them in a single layer on a baking sheet. Roast for 15 minutes, flip and roast for another 15 minutes. Once done, remove from the oven and transfer chicken, artichokes, and juices to a platter. Tent with foil to keep warm.

3. Switch oven to broil. Toss kale with the remaining 1 tablespoon of olive oil. Arrange on the same baking sheet and broil until golden brown and crispy, for about 3 to 5 minutes.

4. Place the crispy kale on top of the chicken and artichokes. Enjoy!

Nutrition: Calories 396, Fat 14.85 g, Protein 19.5 g, Carbohydrates 48.35 g, Sugar 11.18 g, Fiber 9.4 g

68. Sumac Chicken with Cauliflower and Carrots

Prep Time: 8 minutes

Cook Time: 40 minutes

Serving: 4

Ingredients

- 3 tablespoons extra-virgin olive oil
- 1 tablespoon ground sumac
- 1 teaspoon kosher salt
- ½ teaspoon ground cumin
- ¼ teaspoon freshly ground black pepper
- 1½ pounds bone-in chicken thighs and drumsticks
- 1 medium cauliflower, cut into 1-inch florets
- 2 carrots
- 1 lemon, cut into ¼-inch-thick slices
- 1 tablespoon lemon juice
- ¼ cup fresh parsley, chopped
- ¼ cup fresh mint, chopped

Directions

1. Preheat the oven to 425°F and line a baking sheet with foil.

2. In a large bowl, whisk together the olive oil, sumac, salt, cumin, and black pepper. Add the chicken, cauliflower, and carrots, and toss until evenly coated with the spice mixture.

3. Arrange the vegetables and chicken in a single layer on the baking sheet and top with the lemon slices. Roast in the preheated oven for 40 minutes, tossing the vegetables halfway through.

4. Once done, sprinkle the lemon juice over the roasted chicken and vegetables, and garnish with chopped parsley and mint.

5. Serve hot and enjoy a delicious Mediterranean-style meal!

Note: Please make sure the chicken is cooked through, with an internal temperature of 165°F.

Nutrition: Calories 885, Fat 82 g, Protein 23 g, Carbohydrates 13.02 g, Sugar 4.69 g, Fiber 4 g

69. Harissa Yogurt Chicken Thighs

Prep Time: 9 minutes

Cook Time: 23 minutes

Serving: 4

Ingredients

- ½ cup plain Greek yogurt
- 2 tablespoons harissa
- 1 tablespoon lemon juice
- ¼ teaspoon freshly ground black pepper
- 1½ pounds boneless

Directions

1. Mix yogurt, harissa, lemon juice, salt, and black pepper in a bowl.

2. Add chicken to the mixture and thoroughly coat. Allow the chicken to marinate for a minimum of 15 minutes in the refrigerator, but it can marinate for up to 4 hours.

3. Remove the chicken thighs from the marinade and place them in a single layer on a baking sheet.

4. Roast the chicken for 20 minutes, turning them over halfway through the cooking process.

5. After 20 minutes, adjust the oven temperature to broil. Place the chicken under the broiler and cook until it turns golden brown, which should take about 2 to 3 minutes. Keep a close eye on the chicken while broiling to avoid overcooking.

Nutrition: Calories 309, Fat 9.77 g, Protein 17 g, Carbohydrates 36 g, Sugar 9.9 g, Fiber 2.6 g

70. Braised Chicken with Wild Mushrooms

Prep Time: 11 minutes

Cook Time: 28 minutes

Serving: 4

Ingredients

- 1/4 cup dried porcini or morel mushrooms
- 1/4 cup olive oil
- 2–3 slices low-salt turkey bacon, chopped
- 1 chicken, cut into pieces
- 1 small celery stalk, diced
- 1 small dried red chili, chopped
- 1/4 cup vermouth or white wine
- 1/4 cup tomato puree
- 1/4 cup low-salt chicken stock
- 1/2 teaspoon arrowroot
- 1/4 cup flat-leaf parsley, chopped
- 4 teaspoons fresh thyme, chopped
- 3 teaspoons fresh tarragon

Directions

1. Soak the dried porcini or morel mushrooms in boiling water for 20 minutes to soften them. Drain and chop the mushrooms, but save the liquid.

2. In a large skillet or Dutch oven, heat the olive oil over medium heat. Add the chopped turkey bacon and cook until it turns brown and lightly crisp. Remove the bacon from the pan and drain it on a paper towel.

3. Season the chicken pieces with salt and pepper, and then add them to the hot oil and bacon drippings. Cook for 10 to 15 minutes, until the chicken is browned on all sides.

4. Add the diced celery and chopped chili pepper to the pan, and cook for 3 to 5 minutes until the vegetables are softened.

5. Deglaze the pan with vermouth or white wine, using a wooden spoon to scrape up any brown bits stuck to the bottom.

6. Stir in the tomato puree, chicken stock, arrowroot, and reserved mushroom liquid. Bring the mixture to a simmer, reduce the heat to low, cover the pan, and cook for 45 minutes.

7. Add the chopped parsley, thyme, and tarragon to the pan, and cook for an additional 10 minutes until the sauce thickens.

8. Taste the chicken and sauce, and adjust the seasoning as needed with salt and pepper.

9. Serve the braised chicken with wilted greens or crunchy green beans on the side. Enjoy!

Nutrition: Calories 436, Fat 21.3 g, Protein 52.62 g, Carbohydrates 6.08 g, Sugar 1.6 g, Fiber 0.9 g

71. One-Pan Tuscan Chicken

Prep Time: 10 minutes

Cook Time: 25 minutes

Serving: 6

Ingredients

- ¼ cup extra-virgin olive oil, divided
- 1-pound boneless chicken
- 1 onion
- 1 red bell pepper
- 3 garlic cloves
- ½ cup dry white wine
- 2 (14-ounce) can tomatoes
- 1 (14-ounce) can white beans
- 1 tablespoon dried Italian seasoning
- ½ teaspoon sea salt
- 1/8 teaspoon freshly ground black pepper
- 1/8 teaspoon red pepper flakes
- ¼ cup chopped fresh basil leaves

Directions

1. Heat 2 tablespoons of olive oil in a large skillet over medium-high heat. Add the chicken and cook for approximately 6 minutes, stirring occasionally. Once done, remove the chicken from the skillet and set it aside on a platter tented with aluminum foil to keep it warm.

2. Return the skillet to the heat and add the remaining 2 tablespoons of olive oil. Add the onion and red bell pepper and cook for about 5 minutes, occasionally stirring. Then, add the garlic and cook for another 30 seconds.

3. Constantly stir in the white wine and cook for 1 minute.

4. Add crushed and chopped tomatoes, white beans, Italian seasoning, sea salt, black pepper, and red pepper flakes. Allow the mixture to simmer, adjusting the heat to medium, for about 5 minutes, occasionally stirring.

5. Return the chicken and any juices that have collected back to the skillet. Cook for 1 to 2 minutes, stirring occasionally.

6. Remove the skillet from the heat and stir in the chopped basil before serving.

Nutrition: Calories 400, Fat 8.65 g, Protein 35 g, Carbohydrates 46.01 g, Sugar 4.35 g, Fiber 11.8 g

72. Chicken Kapama

Prep Time: 10 minutes

Cook Time: 2 hours

Serving: 4

Ingredients

- 1 (32-ounce) can chopped tomatoes
- ¼ cup dry white wine
- 2 tablespoons tomato paste
- 3 tablespoons extra-virgin olive oil
- ¼ teaspoon red pepper flakes
- 1 teaspoon ground allspice
- ½ teaspoon dried oregano
- 2 whole cloves
- 1 cinnamon stick
- ½ teaspoon sea salt
- 1/8 teaspoon black pepper
- 4 boneless, skinless chicken breast halves

Directions

1. In a pot over medium-high heat, combine the chopped tomatoes, dry white wine, tomato paste, extra-virgin olive oil, red pepper flakes, allspice, oregano, cloves, cinnamon stick, sea salt, and black pepper. Bring the mixture to a simmer while occasionally stirring.

2. Reduce the heat to medium-low and let it simmer for 30 minutes, occasionally stirring.

3. Discard the cloves and cinnamon stick, and let the sauce cool.

4. Preheat your oven to 350°F.

5. Place the boneless, skinless chicken breast halves in a 9-by-13-inch baking dish. Drizzle the sauce over the chicken and cover the dish with aluminum foil. Bake for 45 minutes.

Nutrition: Calories 118, Fat 8.2 g, Protein 4.9 g, Carbohydrates 7.29 g, Sugar 4.35 g, Fiber 1.8 g

73. Spinach and Feta–Stuffed Chicken Breasts

Prep Time: 10 minutes

Cook Time: 45 minutes

Serving: 4

Ingredients

- 2 tablespoons extra-virgin olive oil
- 1-pound fresh baby spinach
- 3 garlic cloves, minced
- Zest of 1 lemon
- ½ teaspoon sea salt
- 1/8 teaspoon freshly ground black pepper
- ½ cup crumbled feta cheese
- 4 chicken breast halves

Directions

1. Preheat your oven to 350°F.

2. Heat the olive oil in a skillet over medium-high heat.

3. Add the baby spinach and cook for 3 to 4 minutes until wilted.

4. Add minced garlic, lemon zest, sea salt, and black pepper, and cook briefly. Then, remove the skillet from the heat and mix in the crumbled feta cheese.

5. Spread the spinach and cheese mixture evenly over the chicken breasts, and roll up the breasts around the filling, securing them with toothpicks or butcher's twine if needed.

6. Place the stuffed chicken breasts in a 9-by-13-inch baking dish and bake in the preheated oven for 30 to 40 minutes.

7. Once done, remove the dish from the oven and let it rest for 5 minutes before slicing and serving.

Nutrition: Calories 425, Fat 20 g, Protein 53.3 g, Carbohydrates 6.46 g, Sugar 1.57 g, Fiber 2.6 g

74. Rosemary Baked Chicken Drumsticks

Prep Time: 5 minutes

Cook Time: 1 hour**Serving:** 6

Ingredients

- 2 tablespoons chopped fresh rosemary leaves
- 1 teaspoon garlic powder
- ½ teaspoon sea salt
- 1/8 teaspoon freshly ground black pepper
- Zest of 1 lemon
- 12 chicken drumsticks

Directions

1. Preheat your oven to 350°F.

2. Prepare the seasoning blend by mixing rosemary, garlic powder, sea salt, pepper, and lemon zest.

3. Place the drumsticks into a 9-by-13-inch baking dish and sprinkle the rosemary mixture over them.

4. Bake the drumsticks in the oven for approximately 1 hour until fully cooked.

Nutrition: Calories 423, Fat 23.9 g, Protein 47.14 g, Carbohydrates 1.33 g, Sugar 0.21 g, Fiber 0.2 g

75. Chicken with Onions, Potatoes, Figs, and Carrots

Prep Time: 5 minutes

Cook Time: 45 minutes

Serving: 4

Ingredients

- 2 cups fingerling potatoes, halved
- 4 fresh figs, quartered
- 2 carrots, julienned
- 2 tablespoons extra-virgin olive oil
- 1 teaspoon sea salt, divided
- ¼ teaspoon freshly ground black pepper
- 4 chicken leg-thigh quarters
- 2 tablespoons chopped fresh parsley leaves

Directions

1. Prepare the Chicken with Onions, Potatoes, Figs, and Carrots, and preheat your oven to 425°F. In a small bowl, mix halved fingerling potatoes, quartered fresh figs, and julienned carrots with extra-virgin olive oil, ½ teaspoon of sea salt, and freshly ground black pepper. Spread the vegetable mixture evenly in a 9-by-13-inch baking dish.

2. Next, rub chicken leg-thigh quarters with the remaining ½ teaspoon of sea salt, and place them on top of the vegetables in the baking dish. Bake for 35 to 45 minutes or until the chicken is fully cooked.

3. Once done, sprinkle the dish with chopped fresh parsley leaves and serve.

Nutrition: Calories 308, Fat 11.04 g, Protein 30.6 g, Carbohydrates 21.5 g, Sugar 6.07 g, Fiber 3.4 g

76. Dijon and Herb Pork Tenderloin

Prep Time: 10 minutes

Cook Time: 30 minutes

Serving: 6

Ingredients

- ½ cup fresh Italian parsley leaves
- 3 tablespoons fresh rosemary leaves
- 3 tablespoons fresh thyme leaves
- 3 tablespoons Dijon mustard
- 1 tablespoon extra-virgin olive oil
- 4 garlic cloves, minced
- ½ teaspoon sea salt
- ¼ teaspoon freshly ground black pepper
- 1 (1½-pound) pork tenderloin

Directions

1. Preheat your oven to 400°F (200°C).

2. In a blender, combine the parsley, rosemary, thyme, Dijon mustard, olive oil, garlic, sea salt, and pepper. Pulse the ingredients until they form a paste.

3. Evenly rub the herb paste over the pork tenderloin and place it on a rimmed baking sheet.

4. Bake the pork tenderloin in the preheated oven for approximately 20 minutes or until it is cooked through.

5. Remove the pork from the oven and let it rest for 10 minutes before slicing and serving.

Nutrition: Calories 308, Fat 11.04 g, Protein 30.6 g, Carbohydrates 1.9 g, Sugar 0.13 g, Fiber 0.8 g

77. Steak with Red Wine– Mushroom Sauce

Prep Time: 10 minutes

Cook Time: 20 minutes

Serving: 4

Ingredients

For marinade and steak

- 1 cup dry red wine
- 3 garlic cloves, minced
- 2 tablespoons extra-virgin olive oil
- 1 tablespoon low-sodium soy sauce
- 1 tablespoon dried thyme
- 1 teaspoon Dijon mustard
- 2 tablespoons extra-virgin olive oil
- 1½ pounds skirt steak

For mushroom sauce

- 2 tablespoons extra-virgin olive oil
- 1-pound cremini mushrooms
- ½ teaspoon sea salt
- 1 teaspoon dried thyme
- 1/8 teaspoon black pepper
- 2 garlic cloves, minced
- 1 cup dry red wine

Directions

1. For the marinade and steak:

2. Whisk the wine, garlic, olive oil, soy sauce, thyme, and mustard in a small bowl. Pour into a resealable bag and add the steak. Refrigerate and let marinate for 4 to 8 hours. Remove the steak from the marinade and pat it dry with paper towels.

3. Heat olive oil in a large skillet over medium-high heat. Add the steak and cook for 4 minutes per side. Once cooked, transfer the steak to a plate and tent it with aluminum foil to keep it warm while preparing the mushroom sauce.

4. After the mushroom sauce is ready, slice the steak against the grain into 1/2-inch-thick slices.

5. For the mushroom sauce:

6. Heat olive oil in a skillet over medium-high heat.

7. Add mushrooms, sea salt, thyme, and pepper, and cook for about 6 minutes.

8. Cook garlic for 30 seconds.

9. Stir in the wine and use a wooden spoon to scrape and fold in any browned bits from the bottom of the skillet. Cook for about 4 minutes.

10. Spoon the mushroom sauce over the sliced steak and serve.

Nutrition: Calories 823, Fat 30.7 g, Protein 56.1 g, Carbohydrates 87 g, Sugar 2.57 g, Fiber 13.3 g

78. Greek Meatballs

Prep Time: 20 minutes

Cook Time: 25 minutes

Serving: 4

Ingredients

- 2 whole-wheat bread slices
- 1¼ pounds ground turkey
- 1 egg
- ¼ cup seasoned whole-wheat bread crumbs
- 3 garlic cloves, minced
- ¼ red onion, grated
- ¼ cup chopped fresh Italian parsley leaves
- 2 tablespoons chopped fresh mint leaves
- 2 tablespoons chopped fresh oregano leaves
- ½ teaspoon sea salt
- ¼ teaspoon freshly ground black pepper

Directions

1. Preheat your oven to 350°F and line a baking sheet with foil.

2. In a medium bowl, wet the whole-wheat bread by running it under water and then squeezing out any excess water. Tear the bread into small pieces and add it to the bowl.

3. To the bowl, add the ground turkey, egg, seasoned whole-wheat breadcrumbs, minced garlic, grated red onion, chopped parsley, mint, oregano, sea salt, and black pepper. Mix well.

4. Form the mixture into meatballs that are about ¼ cup in size, and place them on the prepared baking sheet.

5. Bake the meatballs in the preheated oven for about 25 minutes.

6. Once the meatballs are cooked through, serve and enjoy!

Nutrition: Calories 318, Fat 14.26 g, Protein 33.3 g, Carbohydrates 13.9 g, Sugar 1.65 g, Fiber 1.8 g

79. Lamb with String Beans

Prep Time: 10 minutes

Cook Time: 1 hour**Serving:** 6

Ingredients

- ¼ cup extra-virgin olive oil
- 6 lamb chops
- 1 teaspoon sea salt
- ½ teaspoon black pepper
- 2 tablespoons tomato paste
- 1½ cups hot water
- 1-pound green beans
- 1 onion
- 2 tomatoes

Directions

1. Heat 2 tablespoons of olive oil in a skillet over medium-high heat.

2. Season the lamb chops with 1/2 teaspoon of sea salt and 1/8 teaspoon of black pepper. Cook the lamb in the hot oil for about 4 minutes, until browned. Remove the lamb from the skillet and set it aside on a platter.

3. Add 2 more tablespoons of olive oil to the skillet and heat until it shimmers.

4. In a bowl, mix the tomato paste with hot water. Pour the mixture into the skillet, along with the green beans, onion, tomatoes, and the remaining 1/2 teaspoon of sea salt and 1/4 teaspoon of black pepper. Bring to a simmer.

5. Return the lamb chops to the skillet. Bring to a boil and then reduce the heat to medium low. Cover and simmer for 45 minutes, adding additional water as needed to adjust the thickness of the sauce.

Nutrition: Calories 131, Fat 7.24 g, Protein 10.09 g, Carbohydrates 7.74 g, Sugar 3.1 g, Fiber 2.5 g

80. Greek Lamb Chop

Prep Time: 10 minutes

Cook Time: 8 minutes

Serving: 8

Ingredients

- 8 trimmed lamb loin chops
- 2 tbsp. lemon juice
- 1 tbsp. dried oregano
- 1 tbsp. minced garlic
- ½ tsp. salt
- ¼ tsp. black pepper

Directions

1. Preheat the broiler.

2. In a small bowl, combine the lemon juice, oregano, minced garlic, salt, and black pepper.

3. Rub the mixture on both sides of the lamb chops.

4. Place the lamb chops on a broiler pan coated with cooking spray.

5. Broil for 4 minutes on each side or until cooked to your desired doneness.

6. Once done, remove the lamb chops from the broiler pan and let them rest for a few minutes before serving.

Nutrition: Calories 63, Fat 2.92 g, Protein 8.5 g, Carbohydrates 0.83 g, Sugar 0.12 g, Fiber 0.2 g

81. Chicken with Caper Sauce

Prep Time: 20 minutes

Cook Time: 18 minutes

Serving: 5

Ingredients

For Chicken:

- 2 eggs

- Salt and ground black pepper, as required

- 1 cup dry breadcrumbs

- 2 tablespoons olive oil

- 1½ pounds skinless, boneless chicken breast halves, pounded into ¾inch thickness and cut into pieces

For Capers Sauce:

- 3 tablespoons capers

- ½ cup dry white wine

- 3 tablespoons fresh lemon juice

- Salt and ground black pepper, as required

- 2 tablespoons fresh parsley, chopped

Directions

1. For the chicken, beat the eggs in a shallow dish with salt and pepper. Put the breadcrumbs in another shallow dish. Dip each chicken piece in the egg mixture, then coat evenly with breadcrumbs, shaking off excess.

2. Heat the oil in a skillet over medium heat. Cook the chicken for 5-7 minutes per side or until cooked to your

liking. Use a slotted spoon to transfer the chicken to a paper towellined plate. Cover with foil to keep warm.

3. For the caper sauce, add all the sauce ingredients except parsley to the same skillet. Cook for 2-3 minutes, stirring constantly. Stir in the parsley and remove from heat. Serve the chicken pieces with the caper sauce on top. Enjoy!

Nutrition: Calories 559, Fat 20 g, Protein 76 g, Carbohydrates 14 g, Sugar 11.33 g, Fiber 2 g

LUISA VERNIZZI

Dessert Recipes

82. Strawberries Coconut Cake

Prep Time: 10 minutes

Cook Time: 25 minutes

Serving: 6

Ingredients

- 2 cups almond flour
- 1 cup strawberries, chopped
- ½ teaspoon baking soda
- ½ cup coconut sugar
- ¾ cup coconut milk
- ¼ cup avocado oil
- 2 eggs, whisked
- 1 teaspoon vanilla extract
- Cooking spray

Directions

1. In a mixing bowl, whisk the almond flour, chopped strawberries, baking soda, coconut sugar, coconut milk, avocado oil, whisked eggs, and vanilla extract until well combined.

2. Grease a cake pan with cooking spray, pour the cake batter, and spread it evenly.

3. Bake the cake in the oven at 350 degrees F for 25 minutes or until a toothpick inserted in the center comes out clean.

4. Allow the cake to cool down before slicing and serving.

Nutrition: Calories 237, Fat 19.7 g, Protein 3.92 g, Carbohydrates 12.33 g, Sugar 10.6 g, Fiber 1.2 g

83. Nutmeg Cream

Prep Time: 10 minutes

Cook Time: 0 minutes

Serving: 6

Ingredients

- 3 cups almond milk
- 1 teaspoon nutmeg, ground
- 2 teaspoons vanilla extract
- 4 teaspoons coconut sugar
- 1 cup walnuts, chopped

Directions

Mix 3 cups of almond milk with 1 teaspoon of ground nutmeg, 2 teaspoons of vanilla extract, 4 teaspoons of coconut sugar, and 1 cup of chopped walnuts in a bowl. Whisk the mixture well and then divide it into small cups. Serve the Nutmeg Cream cold.

Nutrition: Calories 160, Fat 10.33 g, Protein 2.81 g, Carbohydrates 15.1 g, Sugar 12.6 g, Fiber 1.4 g

84. Mediterranean Watermelon Salad

Prep Time: 4 minutes

Cook Time: 0 minutes

Serving: 4

Ingredients

- 1 cup watermelon, peeled and cubed
- 2 apples, cored and cubed
- 1 tablespoon coconut cream
- 2 bananas, cut into chunks

Directions

1. Cut the watermelon into cubes and remove the peel. Core and cube the apples. Cut the bananas into chunks.

2. In a large bowl, combine the watermelon, apples, bananas, and coconut cream.

3. Toss the ingredients well and serve the salad immediately.

Note: The preparation time is 4 minutes, and there is no cooking time involved

Nutrition: Calories 160, Fat 10.33 g, Protein 2.81 g, Carbohydrates 15.1 g, Sugar 12.6 g, Fiber 1.4 g

85. Orange Compote

Prep Time: 10 minutes

Cook Time: 15 minutes

Serving: 4

Ingredients

- 5 tablespoons coconut sugar
- 2 cups orange juice
- 4 oranges, peeled and cut into segments

Directions

1. Combine the peeled and segmented oranges with the coconut sugar and orange juice in a pot. Toss the ingredients.

2. Place the pot over medium heat and bring the mixture to a boil.

3. Reduce the heat and let the mixture simmer for about 15 minutes, occasionally stirring until it thickens and the oranges become tender.

4. Remove the pot from the heat and let the compote cool to room temperature.

5. Divide the compote into serving bowls and refrigerate until cold.

6. Serve the cold orange compote as a refreshing and healthy dessert.

Nutrition: Calories 169, Fat 0.36 g, Protein 2.12 g, Carbohydrates 41.9 g, Sugar 32.03 g, Fiber 3.5 g

86. Pears Stew

Prep Time: 10 minutes

Cook Time: 15 minutes

Serving: 4

Ingredients

- 2 cups pears, cored and cut into wedges
- 2 cups water
- 2 tablespoons coconut sugar
- 2 tablespoons lemon juice

Directions

1. In a pot, combine the pear wedges with water, coconut sugar, and lemon juice. Toss the ingredients together.

2. Place the pot over medium heat and bring the mixture to a boil.

3. Reduce the heat and let the mixture simmer for about 15 minutes, occasionally stirring until the pears become tender and the stew thickens.

4. Remove the pot from the heat and let the pear stew cool to a comfortable temperature.

5. Divide the pear stew into serving bowls and serve it as a healthy and comforting dessert or snack.

6. Enjoy your delicious and nutritious Pear Stew!

Nutrition: Calories 116, Fat 0.19 g, Protein 0.29 g, Carbohydrates 30 g, Sugar 24 g, Fiber 2.2 g

87. Cranberry and Pistachio Biscotti

Prep Time: 15 minutes

Cook Time: 35 minutes

Serving: 36

Ingredients

- 1/4 cup light olive oil
- 3/4 cup white sugar
- 2 teaspoons vanilla extract
- 1/2 teaspoon almond extract
- 2 eggs
- 1 3/4 cups all-purpose flour
- 1/4 teaspoon salt
- 1 teaspoon baking powder
- 1/2 cup dried cranberries
- 1 1/2 cups pistachio nuts

Directions

1. Preheat the oven to 150°C.

2. In a large bowl, whisk the olive oil and sugar until well combined. Add the vanilla and almond extracts and the eggs, and mix until smooth.

3. In a separate bowl, combine the flour, salt, and baking powder. Gradually add this mixture to the wet ingredients, stirring until just incorporated. Then, fold in the cranberries and pistachio nuts by hand.

4. Divide the dough in half, and shape each half into a 12 x 2-inch log on a parchment-lined baking sheet. If the dough is sticky, wet your hands with cold water to make it easier to handle.

5. Bake the logs in the preheated oven for 35 minutes or until they are golden brown. Remove from the oven and let cool for 10 minutes. Reduce the oven temperature to 275°F (135°C).

6. Slice the logs diagonally into 3/4-inch-thick pieces, and place the slices on their sides on the parchment-lined baking sheet. Bake for an additional 8-10 minutes or until the biscotti are lightly browned and crisp.

7. Remove from the oven and let cool completely before serving. Enjoy!

Nutrition: Calories 76, Fat 4.38 g, Protein 2.29 g, Carbohydrates 7.2 g, Sugar 1.31 g, Fiber 0.8 g

88. After Meal Apples

Prep Time: 15 minutes

Cook Time: 25 minutes

Serving: 2

Ingredients

- Apple, 1 whole, cut into chunks
- Pineapple chunks, ½ cups
- Grapes, seedless, ½ cup
- Orange juice, ¼ cup
- Cinnamon, ¼ teaspoon

Directions

1. Preheat your oven to 350F.

2. Cut one whole apple into chunks and add it to a baking dish along with 1/2 cup of pineapple chunks and 1/2 cup of seedless grapes.

3. Drizzle 1/4 cup of orange juice over the fruit and sprinkle 1/4 teaspoon of cinnamon on top.

4. Bake the fruit for 25 minutes in the preheated oven, and serve it hot.

Nutrition: Calories 142, Fat 0.32 g, Protein 0.98 g, Carbohydrates 36 g, Sugar 30 g, Fiber 3.5 g

89. Warm Nut Bites

Prep Time: 10 minutes

Cook Time: 20 minutes

Serving: 2

Ingredients

- Honey, 4 tablespoons
- Almonds, 2 cups
- Almond oil, 1 tablespoon

Directions

1. Preheat the oven to 350F and line a baking sheet with parchment paper.

2. Evenly spread the almonds on the baking sheet and bake for 15 minutes, stirring once halfway through.

3. Remove the baking sheet from the oven and drizzle the almond oil over the almonds.

4. Add the honey to the almonds and stir until the almonds are evenly coated.

5. Bake the almonds for 5 minutes or until the honey is caramelized and the almonds are fragrant.

6. Let the almonds cool for a few minutes before serving.

Nutrition: Calories 96, Fat 7.1 g, Protein 0.16 g, Carbohydrates 8.78 g, Sugar 8.65 g, Fiber 0.1 g

90. Hazelnut Cookies

Prep Time: 8 minutes

Cook Time: 21 minutes

Serving: 5

Ingredients

- 1 1/4 cups hazelnut meal
- 6 tbsp. flour
- 1 tbsp. brown sugar
- 2 tbsp. powdered sugar
- 1/2 tsp. kosher salt
- 1/2 lemon zest
- 1/2 lemon juice
- 1/2 tps. vanilla
- 1/4 cup extra virgin olive oil

Directions

1. Preheat the oven to 375 degrees F.

2. In a bowl, whisk together the hazelnut meal, flour, brown sugar, half of the powdered sugar, lemon zest, and salt.

3. In a separate bowl, whisk the olive oil and vanilla.

4. Add the wet ingredients to the dry ingredients and mix until crumbly dough forms.

5. Shape the dough into cookies and place them on a lined baking sheet.

6. Bake for around 20 minutes or until the edges are lightly browned.

7. Allow the cookies to cool on a rack.

8. In a small bowl, mix the remaining powdered sugar and lemon juice to make syrup.

9. Drizzle the syrup over the cookies before serving. Enjoy!

Nutrition: Calories 306, Fat 25.26 g, Protein 6.09 g, Carbohydrates 17.29 g, Sugar 5.5 g, Fiber 3.6 g

91. Honey Yogurt with Berries

Prep Time: 12 minutes

Cook Time: 0 minute

Serving: 2

Ingredients

- 4 oz. hulled, halved strawberries
- 1/6 cup Greek yogurt
- 1/2 cup blueberries
- 1/2 cup raspberries
- 1 tsp. honey
- 1/2 tbsp. balsamic vinegar

Directions

1. In a large bowl, combine the halved strawberries, blueberries, and raspberries with balsamic vinegar.

2. Set the berry mixture aside for 8 to 10 minutes.

3. In a separate bowl, mix the Greek yogurt with honey.

4. To serve, spoon the honey yogurt over the berries.

5. Enjoy your delicious honey yogurt with berries!

Note: This recipe is a great choice for those following a Mediterranean diet, as it features nutritious fruits and protein-rich Greek yogurt.

Nutrition: Calories 156, Fat 0.5 g, Protein 2.83 g, Carbohydrates 37.55 g, Sugar 32 g, Fiber 4.3 g

92. Ricotta Brulee

Prep Time: 7 minutes

Cook Time: 14 minutes

Serving: 4

Ingredients

- fresh raspberries
- 1 cup whole milk ricotta cheese
- 1 tbsp. granulated sugar
- 1/2 tsp. finely grated lemon zest
- 1 tbsp. honey

Directions

1. In a large bowl, mix the ricotta cheese, honey, and lemon zest until well combined.

2. Divide the mixture evenly among four ramekins.

3. Sprinkle a little bit of granulated sugar over the top of each ramekin if you don't have a kitchen torch to caramelize the sugar.

4. Place the ramekins on a baking sheet and put them on the highest oven rack.

5. Turn on the broiler and cook the ricotta until it turns golden-brown and starts to bubble, for about 3-5 minutes.

6. Turn off the oven and let the ricotta cool down.

7. Once cooled, top each ramekin with fresh raspberries.

8. Serve the dessert cold.

Nutrition: Calories 148, Fat 8.25 g, Protein 7.37 g, Carbohydrates 11 g, Sugar 7.81 g, Fiber 2 g

93. Chocolate Quinoa Bars

Prep Time: 19 minutes

Cook Time: 6 minutes

Serving: 10

Ingredients

- 1/4 tsp. vanilla
- 2 oz. semi-sweet chocolate
- 1/2 cup dry quinoa
- 1/2 tbsp. powdered peanut butter
- Peanut Butter Drizzle:
- 1 tbsp. water
- 9 tsp. powdered peanut butter

Directions

1. Heat a large pot over medium heat.

2. Once the pot is hot, add the dry quinoa, 45 grams at a time.

3. Occasionally stir the quinoa until it starts to pop.

4. Once the popping starts, continuously stir for a minute.

5. Once the quinoa has popped, transfer it to a small bowl.

6. Set up a double boiler and melt the semi-sweet chocolate.

7. In a large bowl, mix the melted chocolate, powdered peanut butter, vanilla, and popped quinoa.

8. Spread the mixture onto a baking sheet lined with parchment paper, making it around half an inch thick.

9. Mix water and powdered peanut butter to make the drizzle, then drip it over the chocolate mixture.

10. Swirl the drizzle around with a fork.

11. Refrigerate the bars until they are set, and then slice them into small bars.

Nutrition: Calories 198, Fat 9.74 g, Protein 4.42 g, Carbohydrates 25.2 g, Sugar 9 g, Fiber 2.5 g

94. Pistachio Snack Bars

Prep Time: 17 minutes
Cook Time: 0 minute
Serving: 4

Ingredients

- 10 pitted dates
- 1/2 tsp. vanilla extract
- 1 tbsp. pistachio butter
- 10 tbsp. roasted, salted pistachios
- 1/2 cup rolled oats, old fashioned
- 2 tbsp. unsweetened, applesauce

Directions

1. Puree the pitted dates in a food processor.

2. Add the rolled oats and 123 grams of roasted, salted pistachios to the food processor, and pulse a few times lasting 15 seconds each, until you get a coarse, crumbly consistency.

3. Add the pistachio butter, vanilla extract, and unsweetened applesauce to the food processor and pulse until the mixture becomes sticky and comes together as a dough.

4. Line a standard pan with parchment paper.

5. Place the dough on the pan and use another piece of parchment paper to press it down and evenly flatten it.

6. Sprinkle the remaining pistachios over the dough.

7. Cover with the parchment paper again and freeze the dough for a while before cutting it into 8 equal bars.

Nutrition: Calories 236, Fat 10.6 g, Protein 11.9 g, Carbohydrates 31 g, Sugar 13.3 g, Fiber 8.1 g

95. Oat Berry Smoothie

Prep Time: 4 minutes

Cook Time: 0 minute

Serving: 2

Ingredients

- 1/2 cup frozen berries
- 1/2 cup Greek yogurt milk
- 4 1/2 tbsp. oats
- 1 tsp. honey

Directions

1. In a blender, combine the frozen berries, Greek yogurt, and milk. Blend the mixture until it is smooth and well combined.

2. Add the oats to the blender and blend until fully mixed and smooth.

3. Pour the smoothie into a glass and drizzle honey on top for some sweetness. Enjoy!

Nutrition: Calories 185, Fat 5.6 g, Protein 11.9 g, Carbohydrates 31 g, Sugar 13.3 g, Fiber 8.1 g

96. Blueberry Compote

Prep Time: 10 minutes

Cook Time: 0 minute

Serving: 8

Ingredients

- 1 (16-ounce) bag frozen blueberries, thawed
- ¼ cup sugar
- 1 tablespoon lemon juice
- 2 tablespoons corn-starch
- 2 tablespoons water
- ¼ teaspoon vanilla extract
- ¼ teaspoon grated lemon zest

Directions

1. Add the thawed blueberries, sugar, and lemon juice to the Instant Pot®.

2. Cover the Instant Pot® and set the Manual button, adjusting the time to 1 minute. After the timer beeps, quickly release the pressure until the float valve drops. Press the Cancel button and open the Instant Pot®.

3. Press the Sauté button. Mix the cornstarch and water, then add the mixture to the blueberry blend and cook until it thickens and comes to a boil, which should take about 34 minutes.

4. Press the Cancel button, and stir in the vanilla extract and lemon zest.

5. The blueberry compote can be served immediately or refrigerated until ready to serve.

Nutrition: Calories 185, Fat 5.6 g, Protein 11.9 g, Carbohydrates 31 g, Sugar 13.3 g, Fiber 8.1 g

97. Dried Fruit Compote

Prep Time: 5 minutes

Cook Time: 20 minutes

Serving: 6

Ingredients

- 8 ounces dried apricots, quartered
- 8 ounces dried peaches, quartered
- 1 cup golden raisins
- 1½ cups orange juice
- 1 cinnamon stick
- 4 whole cloves

Directions

1. In the Instant Pot®, combine the dried apricots, dried peaches, golden raisins, orange juice, cinnamon stick, and whole cloves. Stir to combine, then seal the lid of the Instant Pot®. Press the Manual button and adjust the time to 3 minutes.

2. When the timer beeps, allow the pressure to naturally release for about 20 minutes. Then, press the Cancel button and carefully open the lid of the Instant Pot®. Remove and discard the cinnamon stick and cloves.

3. Press the Sauté button and simmer the fruit mixture for 5-6 minutes until slightly thickened. Serve the compote warm or refrigerate it for up to a week.

Nutrition: Calories 174, Fat 0.27 g, Protein 1.74 g, Carbohydrates 45 g, Sugar 36 g, Fiber 2.6 g

98. Cinnamon-Stewed Dried Plums with Greek Yogurt

Prep Time: 10 minutes

Cook Time: 15 minutes

Serving: 6

Ingredients

- 3 cups dried plums
- 2 cups water
- 2 tablespoons sugar
- 2 cinnamon sticks
- 3 cups low-fat plain Greek yogurt

Directions

1. In the Instant Pot®, combine the dried plums, water, sugar, and cinnamon sticks. Close the lid and set the steam release to Sealing. Press the Manual button and set the timer to 3 minutes.

2. Once the timer beeps, quick-release the pressure. Press the Cancel button and carefully open the lid. Remove the cinnamon sticks and discard them.

3. Serve the warm cinnamon-stewed dried plums over low-fat plain Greek yogurt. Enjoy!

Nutrition: Calories 204, Fat 2.04 g, Protein 6.93 g, Carbohydrates 41 g, Sugar 40 g, Fiber 1.6 g

99. Vanilla-Poached Apricots

Prep Time: 10 minutes

Cook Time: 20 minutes

Serving: 6

Ingredients

- 1¼ cups water
- ¼ cup marsala wine
- ¼ cup sugar
- 1 teaspoon vanilla bean paste
- 8 medium apricots, sliced in half and pitted

Directions

1. In the Instant Pot®, combine the water, marsala wine, sugar, and vanilla bean paste. Add the apricots and stir to coat them with the mixture. Seal the lid tightly and press the Manual button. Set the timer for 1 minute.

2. After the timer beeps, carefully quick-release the pressure until the float valve drops. Press Cancel and open the lid. Let the apricots sit in the poaching liquid for 10 minutes. Then, using a slotted spoon, remove the apricots from the liquid and serve them warm or at room temperature.

Nutrition: Calories 64, Fat 0.05 g, Protein 0.4 g, Carbohydrates 16 g, Sugar 15 g, Fiber 0.9 g

100. Creamy Spiced Almond Milk

Prep Time: 10 minutes

Cook Time: 15 minutes

Serving: 6

Ingredients

- 1 cup raw almonds
- 5 cups filtered water, divided
- 1 teaspoon vanilla bean paste
- ½ teaspoon pumpkin pie spice

Directions

1. Add the raw almonds and 1 cup of water to the Instant Pot®. Close the lid and select the Manual option, setting the time to 1 minute.

2. When the timer beeps, quickly release the pressure until the float valve drops. Click the Cancel button and open the lid. Strain the almonds and rinse them under cool water.

3. Transfer them to a high-powered blender, along with the remaining 4 cups of water.

4. Blend on high speed for 2 minutes.

5. Pour the mixture into a nut milk bag set over a large bowl, and squeeze the bag to extract all the liquid. Stir in the vanilla bean paste and pumpkin pie spice. Transfer the mixture to a Mason jar or sealed jug, and refrigerate it for 8 hours. Before serving, gently stir or shake the mixture.

Nutrition: Calories 4, Fat 0.12 g, Protein 0.12 g, Carbohydrates 0.71 g, Sugar 0.4 g, Fiber 0.1 g

101. Zabaglione with Strawberries

Prep Time: 5 minutes

Cook Time: 10 minutes

Serving: 2

Ingredients

- 4 egg yolks, at room temperature
- ½ cup dry marsala
- ¼ cup sugar
- ½ pint strawberries, sliced

Directions

1. In a double boiler, combine the egg yolks, marsala, and sugar.

2. Using a hand mixer on low speed, beat the mixture for 4-7 minutes until it becomes hot and forms a ribbon when the beaters are lifted. Avoid overcooking, as it may cause the mixture to curdle.

3. Slice the strawberries and place them in serving glasses. Top them with the hot zabaglione and immediately serve, or chill in the refrigerator for 1 hour before serving.

Nutrition: Calories 235, Fat 9.9 g, Protein 5.99 g, Carbohydrates 33 g, Sugar 29 g, Fiber 1.8 g

www.ingramcontent.com/pod-product-compliance
Lightning Source LLC
Chambersburg PA
CBHW071151130726
47998CB00002B/474